Don't Blink

Don't Blink

*What the little boy
nobody expected to live
is teaching the world
about life*

BRANDON & BRITTANY BUELL
parents of "Jaxon Strong"

with ANGELA HUNT

Tyndale House Publishers, Inc.
Carol Stream, Illinois

Visit Tyndale online at www.tyndale.com.

TYNDALE and Tyndale's quill logo are registered trademarks of Tyndale House Publishers, Inc.

Don't Blink: What the Little Boy Nobody Expected to Live Is Teaching the World about Life

Designed by Jacqueline L. Nuñez

Edited by Stephanie Rische

Published in association with Folio Literary Management, LLC, 630 9th Avenue, Suite 1101, New York, NY 10036.

Angela Hunt is represented by the literary agency of Browne and Miller Literary Agency Associates LLC, 410 S. Michigan Ave, Suite 460, Chicago, IL 60605.

Library of Congress Cataloging-in-Publication Data

Names: Buell, Brandon, author. | Buell, Brittany, author. | Hunt, Angela Elwell, date, author.
Title: Don't blink : what the little boy nobody expected to live is teaching the world about life / Brandon and Brittany Buell, with Angela E. Hunt.
Description: Carol Stream, IL : Tyndale House Publishers, Inc., 2016. | Includes bibliographical references.
Identifiers: LCCN 2016020295 | ISBN 9781496416520 (hc)
Subjects: LCSH: Parents of children with disabilities—Religious life. | Anencephaly. | Buell, Jaxon, 2014-
Classification: LCC BV4596.P35 B84 2016 | DDC 248.8/6196043—dc23 LC record available at https://lccn.loc.gov/2016020295

Printed in the United States of America

22	21	20	19	18	17	16
7	6	5	4	3	2	1

This book is dedicated to our son,
Jaxon Emmett Buell,
and the strong, brave life he has lived against the
odds every single day . . . which is why his story
has become known as "Jaxon Strong."

I can never escape from your Spirit!
>   I can never get away from your presence!
If I go up to heaven, you are there;
>   if I go down to the grave, you are there.
If I ride the wings of the morning,
>   if I dwell by the farthest oceans,
even there your hand will guide me,
>   and your strength will support me.
I could ask the darkness to hide me
>   and the light around me to become night—
>   but even in darkness I cannot hide from you.
To you the night shines as bright as day.
>   Darkness and light are the same to you.

You made all the delicate, inner parts of my body
>   and knit me together in my mother's womb.
Thank you for making me so wonderfully complex!
>   Your workmanship is marvelous—how well I know it.
You watched me as I was being formed in utter seclusion,
>   as I was woven together in the dark of the womb.
You saw me before I was born.
>   Every day of my life was recorded in your book.
Every moment was laid out
>   before a single day had passed.

PSALM 139:7-16

Contents

Introduction

My wife, Brittany, and I have a small problem. Ever since the birth of Jaxon, our baby boy, we've been deluged with Facebook messages, e-mails, and letters. We hear from people who watched our story on *Nightline*, read about us in the newspaper, or saw our posts and photographs online. Some of them want to give us a long-distance hug of encouragement, and a few want to give us a piece of their minds. Some want to cheer us on because they've been in similar situations, and others want to warn us about the challenges ahead. Some write out of a well of anger or disappointment, but far more write from an ocean of compassion.

I wish we had the time to sit down and respond to each message and answer every question, but meeting the needs of our unique son fills nearly every hour that isn't already required for sleeping, eating, or working.

So we're writing this book to answer all the questions and comments we haven't been able to respond to . . . and perhaps a few that haven't been asked yet. We're writing so you can know why we made the decision to have Jaxon even though we knew he would face serious physical challenges. We're writing so you can know how we felt when he first came into the world and what we thought when medical experts told us he probably wouldn't live more than a few hours after birth. We're writing so you can understand why we're convinced that Jaxon is who he is—and he is not a mistake, because God does not make mistakes. Most of all, we're writing in the hope that our joy can splash from these pages into your life. We adore our son, and we celebrate him for being the marvel and inspiration he is.

We could fill this book with platitudes and some of the cute phrases you often find beneath pictures of wide-eyed kittens dangling from branches. Instead, we'd like to tell true stories about two ordinary people who welcomed an extraordinary child into their home and haven't regretted that decision for a single minute.

Through the tears and the challenges, beneath the struggles and the complications, we have learned a few things about living a life of joy in the midst of challenging circumstances. If any of these life lessons can help you bear your burdens with greater patience, look at your loved ones with new appreciation, or find hope in a desperate situation, then we will have accomplished our purpose.

Brandon and Brittany, for Jaxon Buell

Trust Your Gut

Brandon

You'll never be fully ready; just make the leap.

Perhaps I should start this story at the beginning, before I was married.

I'm one of those rare Florida natives, the son of two schoolteachers. I was pretty much heading nowhere special until I answered a message from a girl on Myspace .com. I'd been raised in a Christian home and my grandfather was a Methodist preacher, so I was never much of a hooligan. But nothing had inspired me to set the bar exceptionally high in the area of personal achievements.

Then in March 2010, I saw the message from a girl named Brittany. The message was about a week old, and I nearly missed it because I was in the process of moving my digital existence from Myspace to Facebook. But I clicked on Brittany's post, and there she was, all cute and blonde and blue eyed. Naturally, I thought it might be worth a shot to give her a call. After all, I wasn't dating anyone at the time. I was out of college, living on my own, and trying to get started in the banking business.

My gut told me to go for it.

Isn't that how it is? When you're not actively looking for something, that's often when you find it.

So I contacted Brittany, who was new in town and visiting a Baptist church in St. Augustine Beach. After a week or two of exchanging messages, I went to church with her, and some of my friends saw right away that this girl and I were never going to be "just friends." After we went out a few times, I could see that she was independent, big hearted, and strong enough not to need me—a quality I found extremely attractive. Even though she was three years younger than I was, she had a certain air of maturity about her.

No one had to hit me over the head—I realized pretty quickly that I'd found a treasure. I'd been praying for a woman who would keep me on my toes, and God had sent her to me via Myspace, proving that He has a great sense of humor.

Brittany and I hit it off, and six months later I asked her to become Mrs. Brandon Buell. We got married on May 1, 2011, and officially began our journey together. We were energetic, eager, and ready to begin building the future we had imagined for ourselves.

When I first met Brittany, I didn't really want children. I was envisioning myself as a successful banker, and kids weren't an integral part of that picture. I wouldn't have minded them, but I was content with just the two of us. I liked being half of an independent couple who could do things and go places at the drop of a hat, and I knew that would change if we had kids.

We *did* make some changes at the drop of a hat shortly after we got married. In 2011, we moved across the state in search of better jobs and more opportunities for career advancement. After moving a couple of times, we finally settled in central Florida, close to where I was born and raised.

After a year or so, Brittany thought it might be nice to have kids, and I was swept along by her optimism. After a few months of trying, the doctor told us that we probably wouldn't have children, so we stopped focusing on getting pregnant. But after a few months, Brittany gave me surprising news: she was pregnant, for real.

Wow. It was an honest-to-goodness miracle. I sat, stunned, as a whirlwind of astonishment whipped through the room. I was happy, excited, and worried, all at the same time. Concerns started popping up in my head like critters in a Whac-A-Mole game. How were we going to take on the additional financial burden of having a child?

Since I worked at a bank, I was always dealing with numbers and bottom lines. My frantic thoughts centered on our financial future—the house payment, insurance, and now the added expense of a child. Not to mention the looming specter of college tuition in only eighteen years . . .

"How are we going to do this?" The words slipped off my tongue before I even realized what I'd said.

"We'll be fine." Brittany squeezed my hand and gave me a confident smile. "Everything's going to work out."

Really?

The timing was crazy. We were getting ready to move into a new rental home, so we were busy packing and trying to organize our lives. As I looked at our list of regular expenses and added to it the miscellaneous costs of moving, I couldn't help thinking about baby clothes, car seats, diapers, and wipes.

I fretted over our budget and analyzed it for a couple of weeks, but eventually I began to relax. It helped that Brittany was completely confident and happy. We moved into our rental house and started settling into a new routine. Life was good. Brittany was ready to enter dental hygienist school, and after that she'd be working full time.

Feeling relaxed and confident about the future, we held hands as we went to the doctor's office for the first ultrasound. Watching that grainy image appear on the screen, I felt a shiver of pure excitement. This pregnancy was actually happening. As the technician moved the scope over Brittany's lubricated belly, we saw little arms, legs, a torso, and a head. Then we heard the baby's steady heartbeat, and my own pulse quickened in response. That was a real, live, beating heart in there, and it was so strong.

Ready or not, we Buells were no longer two, but three.

Sometimes you have to dream it before it becomes a reality.
Until we learned Brittany was pregnant, I'd never dreamed of having a son. I know I would have loved a daughter just as much, but within a few minutes of hearing our baby's strong heartbeat, I began to hope our child was a boy. The more Brittany and I talked about it, the more the idea of having a boy appealed to me.

Maybe I felt that way because although I had an older sister, I was the only boy in my family. Growing up, I was an athletic, "all boy" kind of kid. I played sports, I liked cars, and I earned my share of scraped knees and bruised elbows from roughhousing with the kids down the street.

Sitting in that doctor's office, I began to dream about raising my boy—cheering from the bleachers during his Little League games, taking him fishing, teaching him how to throw a football and catch a baseball.

Brittany and I had already discussed our favorite names, and we were favoring Jaxon Emmett for a son.

Jaxon means "God has been gracious and shown devotion," and Emmett means "hardworking." Perfect!

I envisioned little marks on a doorframe in our house, where we'd record our son's latest growth spurt. Each year we'd stand Jaxon up against the doorframe, measure him, and record the date along with his height—gently, in pencil, so Brittany wouldn't mind.

I imagined Jaxon and me kicking back on the couch and watching a football or baseball game, roaring like lions each time our team scored and giving each other high fives as we did victory dances in the living room. The extended family would come over on weekends, and all the guys would talk sports, our Jaxon chiming in with his cousins as we rooted for the Jacksonville Jaguars, the Pittsburgh Steelers, the Florida State Seminoles, and the Atlanta Braves.

On his birthday, Brittany would decorate our son's cake with miniature baseball and football players. We'd gather around and urge him to make a wish before he blew out the candles. Brittany, of course, would know what he was wishing for, so we'd have the new basketball or bike or scooter in the garage, all ready for him. The neighborhood kids would come over and gaze admiringly at his birthday gift, but we would have taught Jaxon to be polite and share, so he'd graciously let all the other kids play with his gift too.

My thoughts halted abruptly. Who was I kidding? I was talking about a *boy*!

Whenever I got into trouble while I was growing up, my mom always said, "You just wait—one day you're going to have a little you!" If my son was anything like me, he would be strong willed, determined, and curious. He'd probably spend a lot of time in the naughty chair while he was a toddler, and we would probably get called to the school at least a couple of times a year. Little boys are often determined to test the rules, and I was sure our son would do his part to try his teachers' patience.

One thing was certain: if we had a boy, and if he was anything like me, Brittany and I would have our work cut out for us.

∽

Brittany
Be ready to listen to divine promptings.
I had always envisioned myself as a working mom because I'd been working ever since I was a sophomore in high school. I was naturally drawn to the medical field, and over the years I'd worked as a medical assistant, a certified nursing assistant, and a physical therapy technician. I'd always loved science, and the medical field seemed like a natural offshoot of that.

I was born in North Carolina, and I lived there with both my parents until they split up when I was fourteen. They would always drop me off at church, and one Sunday the preacher said, "If you haven't accepted Jesus Christ as your Lord and Savior, feel free to come down front so we can pray with you." I didn't really know why, but I felt this irresistible urge to go to the front. That kind of thing was completely out of character for me. I was never one to voluntarily put myself in front of people, so this prompting to go forward meant something outside myself was responsible. I walked down front and prayed that prayer to accept Christ.

I made it through middle school and high school, with all their ups and downs. After graduation, I was working and living with my dad in North Carolina when one night I had the oddest feeling that God wanted me to move to Florida. Why? I had no idea, but I couldn't shake the thought. Once again, it was like something or someone outside myself was calling me to take action.

I resisted. I told God that I didn't want to move to Florida. My mom lived there, and I didn't necessarily want to live with her. I loved her, but I was twenty-one and no longer a little girl.

The next morning I woke and sat up in bed, hoping that God had moved on to nudge someone else. I looked at the calendar—March 4, 2010—and there it was again, that strong feeling that God was whispering in my ear. *Go to Florida.*

"Why? I don't have a job there. I don't have any friends there. I don't have anywhere to live, except with Mom."

Go to Florida.

Sigh.

What could I do? I had to either go to Florida or get used to waking up every morning with an insistent voice whispering in my ear.

So I quit my job and went to live with my mom in a small town near Daytona Beach. Once I'd unpacked, I spent the first couple of days doing research online. I was looking for friends, male or female, who could introduce me to a good church. I searched Myspace for people who lived in the area and found Brandon's profile. He talked about God in his bio, a fact that impressed me, so I sent him a message.

We messaged online for a couple of weeks, and then we met in St. Augustine, about forty-five minutes north of where I was living. I was a little nervous as I walked up to the beach restaurant where we'd arranged to meet for the first time, but his relaxed manner and his smile immediately put me at ease. I wouldn't have admitted it to Brandon at the time, but I knew this in my gut: God certainly had a plan for me here in Florida.

There are times you need to ignore the experts.

We started trying to have a baby after the first year and a half of our marriage. When I didn't get pregnant right away, I went to a doctor who told me that due to some problems with ovarian cysts and other complications, I wouldn't be able to have children without help. I went through a couple of rounds of hormone therapy to regulate my ovulation, and when that didn't work, we quit trying and just decided to focus on being active and healthy. I worked out a lot—so much that my doctor told me I'd need more fat on my body if I really wanted to have a baby. I cut back on my running, and in January 2014, I discovered I was pregnant.

I had my first ultrasound at eight weeks. Brandon and I were thrilled to see our baby and hear the heartbeat. The fact that I was pregnant seemed like an absolute miracle. We hadn't been able to create a pregnancy when we wanted to, but God had no problem using us to create a new life in His perfect timing.

From a human standpoint, the timing was a little rough, but that didn't do anything to dampen our enthusiasm. My life had become super busy in the last several months, as I was working during the day and going to dental hygienist school at night. I was confident we could make it work, however, especially since I planned to be finished with my classes around the time the baby was born.

The day of the seventeen-week ultrasound arrived, and we couldn't wait to find out the gender of our baby. I climbed onto the table, and the technician squirted my belly with gel and applied the scope. Brandon and I were chattering away when the baby's image appeared on the screen. All at once, the technician got really quiet. A line appeared between her brows, and although she tried to hide her concern, I could tell something was bothering her. She told us we were having a boy, which was great news because we were both hoping for a son. When she was done, she told us she needed to check with the doctor before we left.

As she slipped out of the room, I looked at Brandon. "Something's wrong," I told him. "I feel it."

But then we got the all-clear to leave. We headed home, rejoicing over the news about our baby boy. I told myself that I'd misread the technician's expression and that nothing whatsoever was wrong.

The next day we got a call from the doctor's office. The baby's head was unusually small, the doctor told me, and the ultrasound seemed to indicate that our baby would be born with spina bifida. She would be transferring my file to a clinic for high-risk patients in Orlando, where they had better ultrasound equipment. This would enable them to keep a close eye on my developing fetus.

My heart pounded as I hung up the phone and closed my eyes. I could hardly breathe. I felt as though someone had threatened my baby. What should I do? What did it all mean? I looked at the empty bedroom we'd been planning to use for a nursery. Had we been foolish to even hope for a child? Had we been too confident, or even presumptuous?

To make matters worse, we were studying genetics in my night classes. I went to class and listened to the teacher talk about chromosomes and genetics and birth defects while at the same time our counselor at the high-risk clinic was telling us that our baby might have a genetic disorder. I wondered what I had done—or what *we* had done—to cause a problem with our baby.

"What happened?" I asked my doctor. "Was this my fault? Are our genes defective? Did we do something to cause this?"

The doctor shook her head. "In most cases, no one knows what causes these kinds of problems," she said. "It could be genetic, but it could also be due to a lack of blood flow or oxygen to the developing fetus." In other words, we might never completely understand what had caused a problem with the growth of Jaxon's head.

After some long nights of talking through the possibilities and wrestling with our fears, Brandon and I eventually decided that the *why* didn't matter. Much more important was the fact that God had sent us a child, a unique child. Since God is sovereign, since He controls the planets and the stars and the weather and the hearts of kings, we could certainly trust Him. We *had* to trust Him.

As I went in for my twice-weekly ultrasounds, I trusted my gut and stopped listening to the doctors' warnings. They talked as if I was going to lose the baby at any time, but I didn't believe their dire predictions. After I got to the halfway point in my pregnancy, I told Brandon that our baby was going to be fine. "Yes, I believe something's wrong," I said. "I can see that he's behind in his growth. But I don't care. We're going to have him, and he's going to be fine."

From the seventeenth week through the twenty-third week of my pregnancy, we were given numerous diagnoses of Jaxon's condition—and none of them were right. At the same time, the doctors kept reminding me that I had until twenty-four weeks to terminate my pregnancy. After that, it would be too late under Florida law.

I'll be honest—Brandon and I did have a brief conversation about termination, but only in regard to three specific questions. First, we asked the doctors if this pregnancy would threaten my life in any way. No, it would not, they said. Then we asked if our unborn baby was suffering or in any pain. Again, the answer was no. Finally we asked if his condition would cause him to suffer unavoidable pain after birth. They said no.

"Then we're not terminating," I told my doctor.

We simply couldn't see any reason for ending the life of a baby who might be small but was still growing and developing—a baby who was even now being made in the image of God. His heartbeat was strong. How could we stop that beating heart?

We decided to leave our son in God's hands. If He wanted to take our baby to heaven, it would be His decision, not ours.

Yet our resolution didn't stop my doctor's office from issuing reminders. Every day at work I got a phone call to this effect: "I just wanted to remind you that you have five days to terminate your pregnancy."

"You have four days."

"Only three days to terminate."

They even set up an appointment for an abortion in case we changed our minds. We didn't. We were determined to see this pregnancy through and to usher this child into the world. He was God's gift to us.

Aside from the mysterious condition that was slowing

Jaxon's growth, I had the healthiest pregnancy imaginable. I didn't experience high blood pressure, morning sickness, or any of the usual unpleasant side effects. And because Jaxon was such a small baby, my belly didn't even get very big.

The doctors scheduled Jaxon's delivery for the thirty-seventh week of my pregnancy. To this day I regret letting them do that—I think it would have been better for Jaxon

if I'd gone to term and waited the full forty weeks. But they were assuming Jaxon wasn't going to survive. They didn't think he'd grow much during the final three weeks, so they scheduled my induction for August 25.

I should have listened to my instincts. I learned that day that when you hear a still, small voice telling you to do something different from what everyone else is saying, pay attention to it. It just may be that God is using your gut to speak the truth to you.

When I got to the hospital, they hooked me up to the IV drip that would induce labor. After two days and several rounds of Cervidil and Pitocin, I tried to deliver my son. But as I pushed and strained to bring our baby into the world, Jaxon's respiration dipped to a dangerous level. The doctors determined that the umbilical cord had wrapped around his neck, so they told me to stop pushing. The medical team whisked me off to the operating room for an emergency cesarean.

They transferred me to an operating table, but I wasn't numb yet. I told the doctors that I could still feel my body and nearly scooted off the table to demonstrate, so they upped my meds until my arms and legs began to shake. I felt like I was suffocating, so I tried my best to focus on my breathing. Brandon had been left behind in the mad rush, and I missed having him by my side.

Though my love for science made me want to watch the surgery, the nurses put up a drape that blocked my view of my belly. Unable to do anything else, I stared at the ceiling and prayed that the baby would be okay. Brandon came in, wrapped in a yellow gown, his head covered in a blue cap. His face looked pale beneath the surgical mask. His eyes squinted in an attempt at a smile, but I couldn't focus on him. All I could think about was meeting my son.

I didn't see Jaxon when they lifted him out. Brandon stood to my left, and he didn't say anything at first. He turned to watch the medical team handle the baby, and

I didn't hear anything for a long, scary moment. Then, finally, I heard a tiny squawk.

Brandon turned back to me, and I could tell he was trying to prepare me. "Babe," he said, "his head is really small."

A nurse brought Jaxon over to me. He was tiny—long and skinny—and his head appeared practically flat. I saw a wide face, a pointed forehead, and a pair of squashed-

 looking ears. Yes, his head *was* small. But the rest of his body looked absolutely perfect.

I kissed my little son hello as tears flowed onto my cheeks. "Jaxon," I whispered, still struggling to breathe. "Hello, baby."

"Four pounds even," I heard someone say. "Let's get him to the NICU."

∽

Over the course of my life, I'd experienced a number of situations when I was sure God spoke to me through my gut: when I walked down to the front of a small church as a child, when I felt prompted to move to Florida, and when I sensed that Brandon was "the one." But the strongest instinct I've ever had is that Jaxon is someone special—that God has a plan for his life, even if it's one we never could have imagined ourselves.

Until we had Jaxon, we never realized how completely God controls life and conception. "I knew you before I formed you in your mother's womb," God told the prophet Jeremiah. "Before you were born I set you apart and appointed you as my prophet to the nations" (Jeremiah 1:5). That's one of Brandon's favorite Scriptures, and now that we've seen it play out in our son's life, it's one of my favorites too.

LESSON 2

Uncertainty Isn't Always a Bad Thing

Brittany

Focus on the business of living.

Jaxon spent almost four weeks in the NICU. At first he was hooked up to machines that monitored his heart rate and respiration. It was terrifying to see his little body attached to so many tubes, especially since the medical staff kept warning us that our baby could die at any moment. But he continued to defy the odds.

When Jaxon was a week old, he had surgery to have his gastric tube placed. The doctors expected to put him on oxygen after the surgery, but he came out of the operating room breathing like a champ. And to the doctors' surprise, he never needed oxygen or life-support machines.

Brandon and I should have realized that what we were being told didn't really mesh with what we were seeing. Our baby was supposedly in his final hours, but the boy in the hospital crib didn't look sickly or weak. We recognized his strength—we had heard his steady heartbeat during those ultrasounds—yet Brandon and I tried to prepare ourselves for Jaxon's imminent death. In those first few days of Jaxon's life, we accepted every word the doctors told us. We braced ourselves, believing it was just a matter of time before he succumbed to his condition—which no one had yet defined with any degree of certainty.

Uncertainty, we later learned, can be a good thing. It gave us reason to hope that our son would live.

For nearly four weeks, we remained by Jaxon's side at the hospital almost around the clock. Brandon was able to take six weeks off work, and we barely noticed as the humid Florida days blurred into nights. Unstable postpartum hormones had turned me into me a blubbering mess, and even Brandon was a wreck as we watched Jaxon, prayed over him, and waited for him to die. We didn't want to miss a moment of his life. But after four weeks, he was still breathing, eating, and soiling his diapers like a pro. Aside from his small head and frequent seizure-like movements, nothing appeared to be wrong with him.

A month after his birthday, the doctors discharged Jaxon and sent us home in the care of hospice workers. We kept the hospice service for a day or two, but it wasn't long before Brandon and I faced a crossroad. Either we could stay mentally prepared for our son's death—which placed a sort of emotional distance between our baby and us—or we could focus on his life while hoping and praying for the best.

At that point, we decided to stop thinking about Jaxon dying and instead focus on the business of living. I thanked the people from hospice and told them they were no longer needed. Our little son was behaving just as a newborn should. Except for the fact that his head was undersized and relatively flat, he acted like an ordinary baby on a regular schedule. He woke us up at night, ate, napped, pooped, and peed—what else was a newborn supposed to do? I was pretty sure I could handle him by myself.

A few days later, my determination to do this on my own faltered when Jaxon pulled out his G-tube. I panicked and rushed him to the hospital, where they put the tube back in. As it turned out, the procedure wasn't as big of a deal as I thought, and I started taking nonemergency situations in stride. The more I learned about how to care for Jaxon, the more confident I felt.

Adaptability is a survival skill.
Since I had always imagined myself as a working mom, I tried to go back to work a few months after Jaxon's birth. I was only a couple of classes away from finishing dental school, and I thought I could easily finish school and then get a job.

We took Jaxon to a local day care center operated by professional nurses who would know how to handle his

G-tube and frequent seizures. I thought things would work out, but Jaxon seemed to catch every bug the kids passed around. The first time he caught a cold and developed a runny nose, he couldn't breathe when he slept. Frantic, we bundled him up and rushed him to the hospital in the middle of the night. He was admitted for observation until the infection passed and he was out of danger.

Along with his heightened susceptibility to infections, Jaxon also suffered from terrible reflux. I fed him pumped breast milk for the first four months of his life, and after that, he struggled with the transition to formula. Once on formula, he had to adjust from eating three times a day (bolus feeding) to an almost continuous flow of food through his G-tube. He threw up after practically every meal, often vomiting his medications along with his food.

But he gradually adjusted. And I learned how to schedule his food and his meds so he could ingest his medications without the risk of regurgitation. What good is medicine if you can't keep it down?

After Jaxon caught two infections at the day care center, I realized that I wouldn't be able to finish dental hygienist school—at least not in the foreseeable future. Jaxon needed to remain at home, and no one would care for him like I could. I surrendered the idea of having a dental career and exchanged it for a labor of love: being Jaxon's mommy.

Since the day we brought Jaxon home from the hospital, he has been my focus, my chief concern, my job, and my joy. He is what gets me out of bed in the morning and what sends me to bed every night. He is my baby, and I am his mother . . . and I wouldn't change that for anything.

Know when to let go of your own dreams.

When I was pregnant, my family came to visit us. I was making breakfast one morning, when my sister said, "Don't get used to having a hot breakfast—you're going to miss that when Jaxon comes."

I turned to her in surprise. "I can still have a hot breakfast. I'll just get up earlier."

She laughed . . . and now I know why.

Before Jaxon was born, I didn't fully understand everything motherhood entailed—all the emotions and the responsibilities and the hours of quiet watchfulness. I thought I knew about motherhood—after all, I'd been raised by a mother—but I never dreamed that being a mom would be so all encompassing.

Before motherhood, you struggle to figure out who you are and what you're supposed to do with your life, and then you might add a spouse into the equation. But when you become a mother, you no longer focus on yourself. You are compelled to focus on your child, and sometimes you aren't able to do even simple things like make breakfast or do laundry or run to the grocery store. When you have another person to take care of, it's easy to forget about taking care of yourself.

I still believe that personal care is important. But when our little boy entered my life, my priorities shifted. I realized I have a precious life to guard and love, and my needs now come second. Jaxon's come first.

After a few months, it became clear to Brandon and me that Jaxon wasn't about to die, and we decided to embrace our new "normal." Brandon returned to a regular work schedule, and I figured out how to become Jaxon's primary caregiver.

It's hard to believe that Jaxon is no longer a newborn, but in many ways I can't imagine our life before he became part of our family. The months since his arrival have flown by in a blink of diapers, spit-up, and cuddles, and in many ways our routine is similar to what it was just after we came home from the hospital.

Here's what a typical morning looks like for me. If Brandon is out, I wait until Jaxon is sleeping, put him on a beanbag chair, and then slide it into the bathroom. That way I can be right beside him if he makes an unusual sound or spits up. Because he isn't able to swallow properly, if he throws up, I have to clean up the mess quickly so he doesn't choke on his regurgitated food.

Some families can use a playpen or a gate to keep their babies safe while Mom takes a shower, but those options won't work for us. I need to keep Jaxon within arm's reach so I can be sure he isn't having a seizure or he hasn't stopped breathing.

If Jaxon is awake, I don't shower. I don't dare leave him unsupervised.

Brandon and I depend on each other to keep a watchful eye on our boy even at night. Since Jaxon sometimes throws up in the middle of the night too, we tag-team the night shift. Brandon sleeps from 11 p.m. until 5 a.m. When he gets up at five, he gives Jaxon his medication, and then I'm free to sleep for a couple of hours. I've also learned to snatch catnaps when I can . . . I just hope I don't start napping in restaurants and doctors' officcs!

I know our routine sounds a little crazy, but after we had Jaxon, I understood for the first time how deep and indivisible the bond between mother and child is. Yes, Brandon has the special role of being Jaxon's daddy, but I'm his mommy. I believe my role is to know Jaxon 100 percent—better than anybody else—not only because I'm his mom, but also because I'm with him almost all the time.

I'm eager to fill the role of primary caregiver in Jaxon's life. Someone has to keep track of things like his medical history, insurance co-pays, notes from our many trips to the doctors, instructions about medical equipment, and details about his care. I deal with all of that plus ordinary tasks like making sure we have toilet paper, shampoo, diapers, baby wipes, and clothes that fit our growing boy—as well as having dinner ready at the end of the day. I may not manage a multicourse meal, but I try to get something on the table so we can eat together!

Jaxon's schedule is a bit complicated. He receives medication four times a day, and he needs his meals delivered through his feeding tube. I have to give him his medication, prime it through his MIC-KEY button (the device on the outside of his stomach that allows us to insert food or medication directly into his tummy), and then hold his food until he has digested his medication.

He's currently taking meds to help him digest his formula, along with a muscle relaxer to ease his spasms and seizures, a neural drug for nerve pain, and a sedative that helps him sleep at night amid the constantly firing neurons in his brain stem. He is on medication for practically every part of his body, and the doctors are constantly searching for the right combination of drugs to help Jaxon remain comfortable and calm yet be able to function to the best of his ability. One day we hope to be able to wean him off his meds, but until then, he is happy and healthy and is making steady progress.

I never realized how much a stay-at-home mom does until I became one. This was never my plan, but with Jaxon's unique needs and with all the uncertainties he faces, I feel it's important for me to be a constant for him. And although I don't head to the office each morning, I *am* working . . . more than I ever dreamed I would. But you know what? God had a plan all along, and I love His plan for me. During all those years I worked in the medical field, I picked up knowledge that has served me well as Jaxon's mommy. In His providence, God prepared me for the role I have today, and I'm so grateful for the way He has led me to this place.

Yes, caring for Jaxon is a lot of work and I don't always know what to expect, but I'm so thankful for the role I get to play in his life. In some ways, I feel like Jaxon's assistant. He wouldn't have all the equipment he needs if I didn't fight for him. He wouldn't have his special car seat—the one that doesn't recline in a position that bothers his feeding tube and strains his neck—if I hadn't researched nearly every kind of car seat on the planet. Sometimes the medical companies send the wrong supplies, and I have to be knowledgeable enough to realize when they've sent something that isn't what the doctor ordered. All these efforts require a lot of energy, but I'm happy to work for Jaxon. I love my son, and I'd do anything for him.

That's just what mothers do.

You may find yourself at an unfamiliar place on life's road right now. Maybe you're doing something you never dreamed you'd be doing. Maybe you're wondering if you've made a mistake along the way or if you've taken the wrong fork in the path.

But let me assure you: God hasn't made a mistake. Solomon wrote, "A man's heart plans his way, but the LORD directs his steps" (Proverbs 16:9, NKJV). You may have deviated from *your* life plan, but God has brought you to where you are. The road may be uncertain, but you are not walking alone.

⮞⮜

Brandon
Life is too short for negativity.
Until we had Jaxon, I hardly ever cried. Now the simplest story or a single line in a movie can move me to tears. Being Jaxon's dad has also taught me to live with uncertainty. And that uncertainty has deepened my life. It has deepened my emotions and strengthened my commitment

to my wife and family. It has given me more compassion and a gift I never went looking for: empathy.

If we're in a public place and see another family with children who face physical challenges, Brittany and I can immediately relate to them. Now we have insight into some of the issues they face. We know about seizures, persistent medical bills, and ordinary illnesses that can become life threatening in a matter of hours. We know that time is the most precious commodity on earth. We know about the fear and discouragement that creep in when the doctor says your child is not going to live to see their next birthday. But we also know about hope—the kind that defies any medical prognosis.

Last year Jaxon and I were sitting on the couch watching an ESPN feature about Chad Carr, the five-year-old grandson of Lloyd Carr, the former head football coach at the University of Michigan. When Chad was four, he was diagnosed with an inoperable brain cancer called diffuse intrinsic pontine glioma (DIPG).

A friend of the family came up with the hashtag #ChadTough, and soon hundreds of people were praying for Chad; his parents, Jason and Tammi; and his two older brothers, CJ and Tommy. Shortly after Chad's diagnosis, the family launched the ChadTough Foundation, a nonprofit organization designed to raise funds for the study of DIPG.

In the first six months of the foundation's existence, people donated more than $250,000 for cancer research.

Chad Carr passed away on November 23, 2015, but his short life made a difference in the world . . . and it may make a tremendous difference to other families whose children have been diagnosed with the same disease.

I couldn't get through the ESPN feature without weeping. With Jaxon asleep in my arms, I sat on the couch and bawled, grateful that Brittany was out running errands. I listened as Chad's mother, Tammi, used the same words and phrases Brittany and I frequently used to describe our son: "He's tough." "He's a fighter." "He's our hero."

More than a year earlier, a friend of ours had come up with the idea to create a "Jaxon Strong" Facebook page to celebrate our little son's life—both his victories and his challenges. We have been inspired by Jaxon's inner strength, and we want other people to be encouraged by his life too. He is a sweet boy, but he's also a fighter—he has to be, or there's no way he could have defied so many odds. We know that ultimately God is our source of strength, and He gives us the strength we need for each day.

The page went up in September 2014, and after the page gained a few followers, we started hearing from other families who had been given the same diagnosis. After feeling so alone in our journey, we were surprised to hear how many parents were walking a similar road. According to the Centers for Disease Control, 3 in 10,000 babies are diagnosed with anencephaly, which translates to about 1,200 babies each year in the United States with conditions similar to Jaxon's.[1]

Some people have questioned our decision to let the world know about Jaxon, but with all the horror in the headlines these days, we thought people might like to hear an occasional positive story. All around the world, miracles are happening. Compassion still flows from strangers' hearts, and people—even little babies—are making a difference for the better in the lives of others. That's what the #JaxonStrong movement is all about.

Despite the uncertainties we face every day, Brittany and I pray that Jaxon's story would not only inspire others but also help families who are walking the path we have walked, especially those who start out just as clueless and scared as we once were.

We want our story to give them guidance and hope. That's why we've gone public with Jaxon's story. We're an ordinary family with an extraordinary son, and we're doing our best with what we've been given. We don't expect everyone to understand our family, our fight, our choices, our son, or his journey, and we don't care to argue with those who don't. Our time together is too precious to focus on negativity.

We agree with the late Zig Ziglar: "Be grateful for what you have and stop complaining—it bores everybody else, does you no good, and doesn't solve any problems."

We may not have all the answers for the future, but by taking one day at a time, we're doing the best we can right now.

~∞~

Brittany
It's okay to stamp your foot; just don't wear out your shoes.
Confession time: uncertainty isn't always easy for me to endure. Before Jaxon was born, I went through a time when I was angry with God. Around the time of that seventeen-week ultrasound, when it became clear that something was wrong, I couldn't help but wonder why God was allowing this to happen to me, especially when I'd been such a health nut before I got pregnant. I had been so active, I'd eaten organic food, and I'd tried to avoid anything that wasn't good for me. Medical experts are constantly telling us to eat right, exercise, and avoid smoking, and I'd done everything I was supposed to do. So why had something happened to *my* baby?

"Why me?" I asked God. "I've always been so careful about what I eat and the way I live, so why is this happening to me?"

I was under a lot of pressure at the time—working, attending night school, and going to the doctor's office at least twice a week. Finding out about Jaxon's condition added emotional stress to my already full load, so I suppose anger was a normal reaction. I probably cried a dozen times every day during that tumultuous time.

I'm glad that God isn't offended when humans behave like humans. He is patient and kind, and He understands.

It took some time for me to process all that I was feeling, but eventually I came to realize that my anger was the result of my selfishness. I was angry because *my* plans had been derailed. I had made plans for the future and envisioned myself as a prosperous professional. My anger erupted because I was going to have to surrender my future to God and allow Him to lead me down the path He had designed for me. I had to exchange the certainties I wanted for the uncertainties of a life lived in faith.

Don't we all struggle with that sometimes? We want what we want, and sometimes we're guilty of telling God what's best for us when we pray for this job or that house without adding "Your will be done—no matter what."

Throughout my life I've heard sermons on Psalm 37:4: "Take delight in the LORD, and he will give you your heart's desires." I think sometimes I get the order mixed up: I seek the desires of my heart and promise to delight in God if He gives me what I want. Instead, we're called to delight in Him unconditionally and trust that He'll help us delight in His plans, even if those circumstances aren't what we would have planned for ourselves.

Though my sense of dread didn't completely leave me until after Jaxon was born, it didn't take long for me to get over my anger with God. I knew enough about following Him to know that Christians have their share of misfortunes and sufferings too and that it's through the hard times that we learn to lean on Him. If I was going to make it through the months ahead, I knew I'd have to do a lot of leaning.

I was determined to delight in the Lord no matter what . . . and to trust Him to handle my heart's desires.

I knew that God had purposefully created our baby, so Brandon and I could rest in His purposes. He was in control. Not me, not the doctors—no one else.

Only God.

∞

Brandon
Make room for the unexpected.
I've struggled with bouts of anger over Jaxon's condition too. When I looked at our tiny, four-pound baby in the elevated NICU bed, I seethed with frustration, knowing

that our son was going to die—or so everyone said. Up until he was born, Jaxon had been an idea in my head, but suddenly there he was—a pink, chubby-cheeked, blue-eyed baby who had completely stolen my heart. Why would God take him so soon?

Within a few weeks, I began to see—and trust—that God had a purpose for Jaxon's life. And if Jaxon died, God would have a reason for that, too. God loves those who bear His image, even the smallest and most helpless among us, and His purposes are often hidden from earthly eyes.

The moment I began to trust, my anger began to fade. Faith is the answer to anger and uncertainty, and I felt my anger fading as my faith in God's purpose grew.

Anger is, of course, a natural part of the grieving process, and Brittany and I understood that. So is denial. When Brittany was pregnant and the doctors told us that our baby would probably die very soon after birth, we didn't believe them at first. We knew something unusual was going on with our baby, but after we got past the shock of that realization, we adjusted to the idea that we would be parenting a child with special needs.

When Brittany was twenty-three weeks along in her pregnancy, the doctors changed their diagnosis from spina bifida to Joubert syndrome, a rare genetic disorder that causes abnormal brain development. One of the signs of

Joubert syndrome is polydactyly, the development of extra fingers or toes. On several of Brittany's clinic visits, the doctors turned the ultrasound monitor toward us, tapped the eraser end of their pencils on the surface, and counted the shadowy digits on Jaxon's foot, showing us that he had six toes—two big toes on his left foot. The medical experts were almost completely convinced we were looking at Joubert syndrome. We were prepared for that, and we were fine with it. After all, a child could live with six toes. That wouldn't be a problem.

When Brittany was in the delivery room, everything was going fine until she pushed and Jaxon's oxygen level dropped. Fearing that the umbilical cord was wrapped around his neck, the medical staff left me in the delivery room while they prepped Brittany for emergency surgery.

I had never felt as alone as I did in those moments. The room rang with silence once everyone rushed out, and I was left alone with my fears. I closed my eyes, so worried that I could barely find words to pray. But God knew what I was thinking and feeling. He knew how much I loved my wife and that little baby who was trying so hard to come into this world.

After a few minutes, a nurse came and helped me get ready to go into the operating room. I scrubbed up, put on a gown, and hurried in for the C-section.

The sight of blood on the floor stunned me. Brittany was awake but groggy, and the nurses positioned me at her head while they pulled the baby out. I heard a weak cry, more like an "Ack!" and then saw the medical team whisk the baby over to a table to be examined. I turned and blinked as I studied him—he was tiny, and his head was startlingly small. His skull seemed to fall straight from a point above his forehead to the back of his neck, and he had no hair.

Though the sight of his head was alarming, I couldn't believe this tiny guy was real, alive, and wriggling in the doctor's hands. I watched as the nurses made his little footprints and then cleaned him and swaddled him in a blanket.

Thinking I should prepare Brittany for her first glimpse of our son, I walked over to her and warned her that the baby's head was small. A nurse brought him over, and Brittany kissed him. Then she groggily settled her head back onto the pillow as a nurse took Jaxon away.

It wasn't until I found myself in another room that I remembered the diagnosis of Joubert syndrome. I asked a nurse if I could see Jaxon's feet. She lifted a brow and then gently removed Jaxon's booties. I counted—twice. One, two, three, four, five. Only five toes on each foot and five fingers on each hand. The doctors had been wrong.

In that instant, I learned that even though you may think you know what the outcome of a situation will be, you

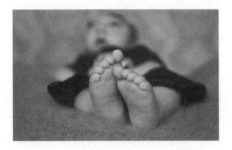

don't really know until it happens. There is always room for the unexpected. Even for a miracle.

As I picked up the certificate stamped with Jaxon's tiny footprints, a familiar saying ran through my mind: "There is no footprint so small that it cannot leave an imprint on the world."

∽

Brittany
Sometimes you walk; sometimes you leap.

I used to think things were usually black or white—you were healthy or sick, employed or unemployed, right or wrong. I thought that you could make plans and see them through, that you could chart a certain course and reach the finish line in due time.

I'm sure you've heard the old saying: "If you want to make God laugh, tell him your plans."

I've come to see that we have very little control over our own lives. Yes, we have control over some things—sometimes.

But never over all things all the time. No human has that kind of power.

In the uncertain world of parenting a child with special needs, life swirls with unknowns. You try to fix your child's problems, but if you can't clearly define the problem, how can you fix anything?

Sometimes you walk a path by faith; other times you leap into the darkness. In either case, you place your faith in the One who has promised to catch you.

When I began dealing with the medical practitioners who were caring for Jaxon, I was quickly reminded why they call it the "practice" of medicine. Nearly all of them were operating by trial and error. The experts took a guess and administered treatment, and if that didn't work, they guessed again or sent Jaxon to someone else.

When Jaxon was nine months old, almost overnight he went from being a happy, contented baby to a miserable, wailing infant. He had been sleeping through the night since he was three months old, but suddenly he began to scream—often around the clock, except for brief periods when he slept after finally surrendering to exhaustion. We tried everything we could think of to soothe him, but nothing worked. He went from being a relatively easy baby to being the most difficult baby you can imagine.

In our efforts to find out what was wrong, we ran

through the usual checklist. Hungry? No, he was being fed. Dirty diaper? No. Teething? He was cutting new teeth, so we gave him a children's painkiller, but that didn't help. Gas? Surely he couldn't have that *all* the time!

Jaxon wailed as though someone were sticking him with a pin, but we couldn't find any reason for his crying. We spent two months visiting doctors—pediatricians, gastroenterologists, and neurologists. I was a nervous wreck, and so was Brandon.

Eventually we had Jaxon admitted to an Orlando hospital so he could be examined from head to toe, but after a week, even the experts hit a dead end. The doctors checked Jaxon's entire body—ears, lungs, sinuses, digestive system—and no one could determine why our baby was screaming all the time. After repeated blood tests, scans, and X-rays, the doctors couldn't give us any answers. Finally the frustrated staff suggested that we take our wailing baby home and make the best of a difficult situation. We weren't satisfied with that.

We desperately wanted—*needed*—another opinion, but we didn't know where to go next. Our home was chaos. I was getting only an hour or two of sleep each night, and we couldn't do anything except tend to Jaxon. One morning I caught a glimpse of my reflection and realized that I looked like the walking dead—tired and pale, with bags under my eyes. I was exhausted. And for the first time since we left the hospital, I found myself thinking we might actually lose our son. What hurt me most was thinking we might lose him without understanding why.

Then Brandon suggested that we take a bold leap and consult the best of the best. We heard that Boston Children's Hospital is the nation's leading hospital for infant neurology, so the day after leaving the Orlando hospital, we flew to Boston. We didn't have an appointment, and we didn't have a definite place to stay. Our plan was to present Jaxon in the emergency room and hope that they'd admit him for tests.

Desperation flew with us as we traveled north. Fortunately for us (and everyone else aboard the plane), Jaxon is an awesome flyer and slept most of the trip. The people around us gave us sympathetic smiles and boosted our spirits. I began to think that heading to Boston was exactly the right thing to do.

We were drained by the time we landed at the airport, but we went straight to the hospital and entered the emergency room. With Jaxon in my arms, I walked up to the desk and said, "Hey, we are here from Florida. We were in the hospital there for a week with no answers, and we need your help. Now." The staff took Jaxon immediately; we didn't even have to wait.

We spent the first few nights with my family in Rhode Island, and then we checked into a hotel in Boston so we could be closer for Jaxon's appointments. Brandon and I relaxed—as much as we could—because we finally felt as though we were making progress. We heard it often takes months to see certain specialists, but because we'd been aggressive in seeking treatment for Jax, we'd managed to book an appointment with Dr. Heather Olson, a neonatal neurologist, only ten days out.

As we waited for our appointment, we decided to enjoy Boston. The weather was gorgeous—it was in the seventies and eighties during the day and cooler at night, a welcome treat for us Floridians. By the time we'd moved to the hotel, it was almost Jaxon's first birthday.

We were taking things one day at a time, and we had no idea what to expect in the coming days. We wanted to make Jaxon's first birthday special, so we took him to see the animals at the New England Aquarium. We bought him a stuffed sea turtle that remains in his room as a symbol of that significant one-year benchmark. The little boy no one thought would leave the hospital somehow made it to his first birthday.

Since that unusual ultrasound at seventeen weeks, we were given several diagnoses for Jaxon's condition, including spina bifida, Dandy-Walker syndrome, and Joubert syndrome. Right after Jaxon's birth, the doctors said he suffered from anencephaly (the absence of a portion of the brain), lissencephaly (smooth brain), and "an unknown extreme brain malformation" that they weren't even able to name.

None of those were accurate diagnoses.

After examining Jaxon, Dr. Olson finally gave us the correct diagnosis for our son's condition: microhydranencephaly. The word comes from *micro* (small) plus *hydra* (water) and *encephal* (of the brain). Where most people have a left and right hemisphere of the brain, Jaxon has spinal fluid. The brain he does have is one-fifth the size of a normal brain.

As we did more research, we learned that children with Jaxon's condition often go through an "irritability phase"—the result of neurons constantly firing. However, medication could help him. Dr. Olson prescribed gabapentin, a drug developed as an antiseizure medication, and it eased Jaxon's discomfort considerably.

Dr. Olson did more than lessen our son's nerve pain— she also gave us hope. She told us that other children with microhydranencephaly have survived childhood and moved into adulthood.

Recently the *Tampa Bay Times* featured a front-page story about a Florida family whose son Anthony Barbaro was born with microcephaly, a condition similar to Jaxon's, and is now forty years old. Anthony wasn't expected to live more than two weeks, but ever since birth, he has gone almost everywhere with his parents. "It was hard at first," Anthony's father, Vince, told a *Times* reporter. "But we loved him."[2]

We will forever be grateful to Dr. Olson for renewing our hope about Jaxon's future. Once the medications began to take effect, he became an easy baby again. The correct diagnosis, coupled with the right medications, eased his irritation and our frustration.

After we returned home from Boston, we followed up with Dr. Carl Barr, Jaxon's regular pediatric neurologist in Orlando. After reviewing Jaxon's records, Dr. Barr acknowledged that there are few certainties when dealing with situations like our son's. Since so few babies with this condition survive more than a few days outside the womb, few cases have been studied.

As he looked at our son, Dr. Barr smiled. "Jaxon is writing his own story," he said, "and we're just along for the ride."

Don't give up, even when the prognosis looks grim.
Before we had Jaxon, we thought the doctors had all the answers. Since Jaxon arrived, we've met some wonderful doctors and a few others who gave up too quickly on our son.

Just after Jaxon was born, one doctor kept reminding us that our baby wouldn't live forever. "How much do you really want to do for him?" the doctor asked. He didn't want to go through with a procedure that would make it easier for us to feed Jax. At one point we asked for a chest X-ray, but the doctor resisted. And when Jaxon went through his irritability stage, that same doctor looked at us and asked, "How much more are you going to put him through?"

I stared right back at him. "I don't understand why you wouldn't want to try everything to keep him with us."

When Jaxon was three or four months old, after we'd done some research ourselves, we met with a geneticist in Orlando and expressed our hope that Jaxon would live several years. She responded by saying bluntly that Jaxon wouldn't make it to his second birthday.

Then, just before Jaxon's first birthday, when no one could find an answer for his irritability, one doctor said we should just take him home and give him "comfort care." He looked at us with a long, somber face and said there was nothing he could do for us. We were not ready to give up—we asked them to discharge Jaxon so we could try something else.

It has been frustrating at times to see medical experts surrender too quickly. There's nothing that will get me riled up quite like when I see medical professionals who have bought into the idea that a "less than normal" life isn't worth living. I'm sure they are under pressure from insurance companies and hospital bean counters, but what has happened to the belief that life is sacred and should be preserved if at all possible?

We have learned this lesson along the way: sometimes you have to keep fighting for hope, even when no one else will. And that may mean walking away from one doctor and finding another who will listen.

We are grateful for the specialists in Boston who are eager to have us check in with them to see how Jaxon is doing. The team at the Children's Hospital is fascinated by Jaxon and encouraged by the progress he's making. They want to follow him because they believe his life will have meaningful impact on the world and on the medical community.

If you are faced with a desperate situation, medical or otherwise, you are not alone. The future may seem bleak and the odds may be stacked against you, but know this: sometimes you have to push back. Maybe you won't get anywhere with the experts, but maybe you will. Push until you get the answers you need, and don't hesitate to ask for a second (or third) opinion.

If a physician is offended by your request for a second

opinion, that's a sure sign that you need someone else. When it comes to finding the right health care providers for your child, it doesn't matter whether they believe your child is capable of living a normal life span. They should respect your right as a parent to do anything and everything for your child's sake. If you and your doctor are not on the same page, then it's time to find a new doctor.

Health care providers—doctors, nurses, researchers, technicians, midwives, surgeons, and physician's assistants—are gifts from God. But they are not God, so they are not infallible. Never forget that these men and women, dedicated as they may be, are engaged in the *practice* of medicine.

Though we no longer work with the geneticist who told us that Jaxon wouldn't make it to his second birthday, we are planning to invite her to his second birthday party. We hope she comes to celebrate with us and hold the baby who has proven her wrong. And we hope that the next time she is sitting in a closed-door session with the parents of a young child, she'll think twice before making such a harsh and negative prediction. All she will have to do is think of Jaxon . . . and remember that projections and probabilities are not set in stone.

We never would have chosen a life filled with so much unpredictability and so many uncertainties. There is so much we don't know about Jaxon's health and about his future. But the truth is, even if he didn't have microhydran-encephaly, we still wouldn't have any guarantees. Life is a gift, but it's an uncertain gift. So all we can do is embrace the beauty in the midst of the uncertainty, knowing that's the best groundwork for a miracle.

Don't Compare Yourself to Others

Brandon
Normal is overrated.

Before we had Jaxon, we never thought much about the word *normal*. It wasn't something that came up very often, and when it did, it was just an ordinary word.

Now we hear questions, mostly from well-intentioned people, who ask if our son will ever be normal. One thing we do know for sure: he will never be an ordinary child. After seeing how God is using Jaxon just the way he is, even as young as he is, I doubt that God will miraculously give Jaxon a full brain someday.

Others question if a life that isn't "normal" is worth living at all.

Well . . . what *is* normal? Does such a state really exist? Most people have brain function that falls into an average range, and we all use our full brains during the day. (The belief that we use only 10 percent of our brainpower is just an old wives' tale. We don't use our entire brains all the time, but we do use our entire brains *some* of the time.)

Some people are exceptionally good in some areas—

computing numbers or linguistics, for example—and we all have decided weaknesses in other areas. I daresay that no two brains are identical, and no one's individual skill sets are perfectly matched. But even though we are all limited in certain ways, don't we learn to compensate for our limitations? We all have differing gifts and abilities. If we're weak in one area, we learn to excel in another.

Every person is unique; every family is different; every child is special. So why not celebrate our uniqueness?

Our family lives with what psychologists call a "new normal." We took "normal" and adjusted it to fit our situation. And our new normal suits us very well.

Our son is normal in so many ways. He cries when he's hungry, he feels discomfort when he's teething, he grumbles with gas pains, he throws up, he fusses, he poops, he pees, he sleeps, and he repeats. For our family, it's normal to feed our baby via a gastric feeding tube. It's normal for us to tenderly embrace him when he has a startle seizure, as he does several times a day. It's normal for us to look at Jaxon and see a perfectly beautiful little boy while other babies look strangely oversized. It's normal for us to take Jaxon out in public and face the pressure of strange looks, stares, and surprised glances—usually from people who aren't even aware that they're staring.

Though some of our practices might be unusual, we

are a normal family, so we have to venture out to refill the pantry, run errands, and grab a bite to eat because we didn't have time to cook or because we didn't want to on a Friday evening.

People frequently ask us if Jaxon is ever going to walk, crawl, and hit other "normal" milestones. We don't know what he'll do, and we have no expectations about when or if he'll reach those benchmarks. We tend not to worry about the future because he's already doing so many things he shouldn't be able to do. All we expect is that Jaxon will continue to strive and achieve what he wants to achieve. Our job is to honor his efforts and encourage him in all the ways we can.

Occasionally people ask if it bothers us to be around other children who are doing "normal" things. When our niece, who is two months younger than Jaxon, began to do things Jaxon couldn't do, it was hard on us at first—especially on Brittany. She'd find herself thinking, *I wish Jaxon could do that* . . . But now when she sees our sweet niece laughing and walking and playing, she tends to think of "normal" activities as simply routine.

"What do parents of normal kids get excited about?" Brittany once asked me. "We get excited about everything!"

We get excited about new noises, giggles, and open

hands instead of tight fists. We are overjoyed by signs of chewing and swallowing. We are tickled when Jaxon eats something he's never tried before.

One night when he was six months old, Jaxon lay in his crib next to us while Brittany and I were in bed. Then we heard him call "Ma-ma!" We both sprang up to check on him, delighted at what we'd heard. We'd been told that Jaxon would never talk at all, but he said "Mama" even before most healthy babies begin to talk.

Since then we've also heard him call for Daddy—though it sounds more like "Addy"—and we've also caught him on video saying "I love you" after I cooed "I love you" to him first. Even if he is only parroting our words, who would have believed he would ever imitate speech?

Once I showed Jaxon some drawings that had been sent by children who are Jaxon Strong supporters in Germany. "Can you say hello to them?" I said, picking up my phone to record his response. Jaxon grinned, worked his mouth, and then crowed, "Hello!" I was thrilled.

What does your family get excited about? What are some of the things your child does that others might consider unusual? There are probably some areas where you and your family don't look like everyone else, and that's okay. How have you adapted to your "new normal"?

Maybe your child has an anxiety disorder, so you have to reserve a special place in the toothbrush holder for his toothbrush. Perhaps your spouse has OCD and can't sleep until he or she has walked a particular pattern through the house and checked the locks three times. Maybe your child is terrified of dogs or a certain color or darkness, and you take unusual measures to be sure nothing in the house will frighten your child.

We go to remarkable lengths to protect and support our family members because we love them. That is "normal" for us.

We have no idea where Jaxon will excel one day or what the impact of his life will be, but Brittany and I know he's strong, and we're convinced his life is worth living. Every life is created in the image of God, and that's something no one has the right to take away or deny. Our world may neglect that principle, but God doesn't.

The first book of the Bible explains how God created human beings: "God said, 'Let us make human beings in our image, to be like us. They will reign over the fish in the sea, the birds in the sky, the livestock, all the wild animals on the earth, and the small animals that scurry along the ground.' So God created human beings in his own image" (Genesis 1:26-27).

At Creation, God looked at the beautiful planet He had made—the majestic oceans and mountains, the fields and trees and flowers, the animals, and the two humans. And He gave human beings dominion over the earth and the animals. People were to rule the earth just as God ruled over them. Humans were to be God's representatives, His image bearers.

That means that even the weakest human being, the smallest and the most helpless, is one of God's image bearers. A person of great worth. And of infinite value in the eyes of God.

∽

Brittany
Different doesn't mean "wrong."
Before we had Jaxon, we were never the sort of people who attracted stares from others. Now we get curious glances pretty much anytime we're out in public.

I know Jaxon's head looks unusual, and I'm not offended when people notice my beautiful boy. I don't even mind when they stop to ask questions, even when they're not sure what to say.

One of the most common questions we receive is

"What's wrong with his head?" I'm happy to answer with an explanation about microhydranencephaly, as long as I have the time. But what I want to say is that there's nothing *wrong* with his head. His head is exactly right for him, because God formed his head this way for a purpose. That purpose may not be obvious to everyone, but Brandon and I are convinced that our son is just the way God intended him to be.

One day when I was shopping at my local grocery store with Jaxon, the manager stopped us as we were leaving. Overflowing with good intentions, she smiled and said, "You know, my mom told me to be sure to turn my baby when he was sleeping so his head wouldn't get stuck like that."

I tried to explain about microhydranencephaly, but I don't think my answer registered. After all, the explanation is a lot to absorb in one dose. But the next time we were in the store, she asked how Jaxon was doing, and I appreciated her concern.

Since Jaxon received quite a bit of media attention when he reached his first birthday, people sometimes recognize us when we're at a restaurant or in the store. They want to stop and talk for a while, and although I'd like to answer all their questions, sometimes I just want to grab a sandwich or a loaf of bread and hurry home.

I understand that anyone who looks different is likely

to get a reaction from people—that's just human nature. But if you ever find yourself staring at an unusual-looking person, remember to attach a smile to that stare. We don't mind if people look at us. Stares are a bit of a turnoff, but smiles are always welcome. Questions are welcome too, because we love to talk about our boy. If you see us and want to know something, feel free to ask, and we'll probably talk longer than you want us to.

I know it can be uncomfortable to start a conversation about someone who doesn't look like everyone else. If you're not sure what to say, the best question you could ask any parent of a child with special needs is this: "What's your little guy's (or girl's) story?"

We'll be happy to tell you.

⚮

Brandon
Never forget that everyone has a story.
Before we had Jaxon, whenever I looked at someone I didn't know, I saw an anonymous stranger. Now I see a person with his or her own unique story.

A friend told us about *Alex: The Life of a Child*, a made-for-TV movie about sportswriter Frank Deford, whose daughter Alex was born with cystic fibrosis. Alex struggled with the disease throughout her short life, and on her final day on earth, as she lay dying, she asked her father for root beer. Her father immediately drove to the grocery store to get some. There's a scene in the movie where the father is standing quietly in line with a bottle of root beer while another customer ahead of him is arguing with the cashier over the price of an item. Can you imagine how that father must have felt? I don't have to see the movie to empathize with the anguish he must have experienced. Seconds of his precious daughter's life were ticking away while an oblivious customer fussed over a few cents.

Since Jaxon arrived, Brittany and I have become much more sensitive to the people around us. We see people our age and wonder if they have children at home and if those children are struggling with health issues or emotional problems. We see middle-aged people and wonder if they've been through a situation similar to ours. We see older people and wonder if they've stood beside the hospital bed of one of their grandchildren. What obstacles have they overcome, and how have they coped with their challenges? Have they been blessed to live relatively ordinary lives? Probably not. Everyone, it seems, faces struggles of one kind or another. But most of us hide our challenges from all but our most intimate friends.

Now that our lives have settled into a routine, Brittany and I are working to get back to a healthy lifestyle. The other day I popped into the gym for a quick workout, and on a nearby treadmill I saw an elderly gentleman who was barely moving. He was probably going at a speed of a half a mile an hour. The "old me" would have laughed to myself at the sight, wondering why he was wasting his time on a barely moving treadmill. But the new me wondered what that gentleman had been through in his lifetime. How had he become convinced that he needed to stay mobile? What if he'd been injured serving our country? Had he been an athlete at some time in his life? How had he found the courage to work out in a gym filled with younger, more athletic people? I doubt thoughts like these would have occurred to me in the "before Jaxon" years.

Have you taken the time to look, *really look*, at the people around you? Do you know your neighbors? Do you know if the older woman down the street has children or grandchildren? What about the young couple across the road? What are their burdens? Believe me, everyone has at least one. If by some chance you know someone who doesn't have a problem in the world, just give them time. Hardship and sorrow catch up to all of us. But tough times don't have to break us—they can strengthen and fortify us. They can lead us to maturity and wisdom, if we let them.

When people meet Brittany and me, they don't guess at first that we face such significant challenges with our child. We usually try to maintain a positive attitude, but sometimes it's impossible to hide our frayed emotions and private sorrows. We've learned that when things get rough, you just have to feel those difficult emotions until you don't feel them anymore. And that's okay.

Jesus wept when His friend Lazarus died, even though He knew Lazarus was about to be raised from the dead. Jesus took time to get away and feed His soul, even slipping away from His closest friends. He made the most of every moment, being fully present in whatever He was doing, connecting with people, and embracing whatever emotion He was facing. He wasn't trying to compare Himself to the religious leaders or keep up with the expectations of the people around Him. Instead, He knew what He'd been called to do, and He devoted His life to fulfilling that call.

I try to post to our Facebook page every day or so, which means I'm frequently looking at pictures of Jaxon. The camera catches him in a microsecond, so people see his big blue eyes, his little smile, and his blond curls. Video clips capture his little chirps, his crows of delight, and his enthusiastic attempts to repeat "I love you" and "hello" after us.

But pictures and videos don't tell the entire story. They don't capture his pain or our fears about how a common cold could result in a life-threatening infection for him.

We don't want to dwell on the hardships, however, because ultimately Jaxon's story is one of encouragement. While we are honest about the difficulties we've faced and the challenges that may lie ahead, our primary message is one of hope. Life is a precious gift from God, and we want to celebrate every minute of it.

Now that I'm aware of how many people are living out difficult stories just below the surface, I find myself more sensitive to what they may be going through. So now when I'm at the grocery store and notice that the woman in front of me has twenty items in the ten-item express lane, I wonder what sort of family emergency is forcing her to bend the rules and rush home. Maybe she has a sick child or an impatient husband. Maybe she's under pressure and simply forgot the express-line limitation.

Whatever her reason, I'll do my best to be patient with her. Because she, too, has her own story.

∾

Brittany
You don't have to walk this journey alone.
Even though each person has a unique story, we also share many things in common. Before we had Jaxon, we didn't know any families with children who have special needs.

We knew they existed, of course, but we didn't know any of them personally.

Now we're part of a whole community of families with extraordinary children. We connected on Facebook through a page intended for families with children who face diagnoses of lissencephaly. Even though Jaxon's diagnosis changed, I still keep in touch with those moms. We share our struggles, our needs, and answers we've found to common problems. For example, one of my mommy friends found a cute container to hold the syringes we use every day to dispense medications, so she shared that news with us via Facebook. When another child first got his MIC-KEY button, his mom was able to reach out for help about how to use the portable bag that holds formula.

I've had dinner and lunch with a few of these mommies and their special babies in Orlando. Since so many families vacation in Florida, it's often easy for us to meet and share our lives. Even if it's our first encounter, we feel like old friends because we have so much in common.

We've become particularly close to two families who live in Orlando. Even though our lives are busy, we make a point of staying in touch, sending pictures of our kids, and sharing news about milestones they've reached. We've even celebrated our children's birthdays together. During the hard times, we ask one another for support and prayer.

Through the Facebook group, we also bonded with a family who lives in New York. We were able to meet up with them when we went to visit my mother in Rhode Island. We had dinner together and spent the night talking—discussing our doctors, sharing advice about equipment, and celebrating our babies' milestones. We don't have to be in daily contact to remain close; our concerns about our children have bonded us.

When you find yourself facing an unusual challenge, particularly with your child, it can be daunting at first. Some people are scared of "different," and even well-intentioned people may not understand it. That's why it's important to find your people—so you can both give and receive support.

As young as he is, Jaxon has already taught us a couple of important lessons about being different: that we have our own unique story to tell and that we don't have to live out our story alone.

Everyone Needs a Little Help
Now and Then

Brittany

Be strong enough to give help—and accept it.

I love caring for my son, and that's pretty obvious to the people around me. But even so, I've been told on occasion, "You're going to need help, or you'll crack under the strain!" I *do* have help with Jaxon—not every day, but some friends have been gracious enough to come over and help with whatever needs to be done. Brandon's parents live nearby, and they come to our house often and lend a hand. I don't know what we'd do without the friends and family who consistently pitch in on our behalf.

Jax also has professional assistance on occasion. A nurse sometimes comes for a few hours, and Jaxon has physical and occupational therapists who guide him with his developmental milestones. These windows give me time "off duty," when I can exercise, run errands, or just catch up on laundry.

Before we had Jaxon, Brandon and I didn't realize how exhausting and expensive it is to care for a baby. Even though we knew about car seats and diapers, we didn't anticipate the expense of a steady stream of formula and wipes and all the miscellaneous costs associated with a baby. Add to that the extra expense of Jaxon's medicines and special equipment, plus the loss of my income, and we were pretty overwhelmed at first.

We quickly discovered that God is more than able to supply our financial needs through the generosity of other people. We were a little hesitant to make our needs known at first—after all, nearly everyone needs financial help these days—but one of Brandon's former colleagues established a GoFundMe page for us. He set as a goal the amount we estimated I might have brought in if I'd been employed as a dental hygienist. Within a few months, generous people from all walks of life helped us not only meet but surpass that goal. We were amazed and humbled to think that so many people—even some we'd never met—were willing to give their hard-earned money to help us.

We are serious about being good stewards of the money people have generously donated to us, so we use it for Jaxon's equipment and medications, and sometimes we use it to help other people as well. For example, the other day we heard about a young single mother whose car needed repairs. We were thrilled to be able to send her the money to cover the bill. We know God controls all the treasures of the world, and He provides for the needs of His people. He also allows us the great privilege of being His hands to serve others.

Since our needs have been so generously met, we've also been able to use the overflow funds to help support nonprofits that work with children and families, and organizations that are involved with neurological research. Jaxon is a daily reminder that children like him need help, and we're so glad to be able to contribute to those causes.

In some ways, Jaxon's slow growth is a blessing. His special car seat was expensive, but due to the side effects of his condition, he won't outgrow it for years. He's still wearing infant clothes, and just graduated to the nine-to-twelve-month size. People have been so generous in giving us clothing, strollers, and car seats, and if we don't need them, we pass them on to someone else. We appreciate all the gifts, and we're glad to be able to pay it forward when we can.

We have learned that wealth is here today and gone tomorrow. Some of the richest people in the world are bankrupt within a few years. Why? Because they didn't invest wisely—and I'm not talking about stocks and bonds. Christians are told to be good stewards of all that God gives us, and that means our finances are to be carefully invested, wisely spent, and joyfully shared with others.

Money isn't to be hoarded; it's to be used in ways that honor God. "Honor the LORD with your wealth and with the best part of everything you produce," Solomon wrote. "Then he will fill your barns with grain, and your vats will overflow with good wine" (Proverbs 3:9-10). We honor God when we joyfully obey that supernatural nudge when we hear about others who need financial help.

God said it is more blessed to give than to receive, and we believe that with all our hearts. We have been entrusted with donations from so many compassionate and loving people, and we try to honor their trust by blessing others as the Spirit leads us. That is one of our greatest joys.

Having been both the recipients and the givers of financial gifts, we have experienced the gratitude that comes from having our needs met and the joy that comes from sharing the abundance we've been given. That's why I encourage anyone who needs help to not be shy about asking for it. We're not shy about asking God for help, are we? Why, then, should we be slow to ask His children? And when people come to us for help and we feel the Spirit of God nudging us to give, let's not be slow to offer what God gave us in the first place. After all, God loves a cheerful giver.

∼∞∼

Brandon
Don't feel guilty for needing a break.

Until we had Jaxon, Brittany and I took our time together for granted. Once Jaxon arrived, however, we didn't have time for date night—or anything close to it. Our family and friends tried to come over so we could take a break, but they weren't familiar with how to handle Jaxon's G-tube and some of his other specialized equipment, so they were a little uncomfortable caring for him alone. They loved him, but these nights out could be a little nerve racking for them—and for us.

When we did find a family member who was comfortable enough to watch him, we were able to go out and take some time for ourselves. But there was a certain price to pay, as it took Brittany nearly all day to get ready for the big event. She had to prepare Jaxon's food and formula, and then she wrote out detailed instructions for working his pump and administering his medications. She felt a little bit like a teacher preparing lesson plans for a substitute, and she found herself wondering if the brief time away was worth all the trouble. Sometimes it is.

In one sense Jaxon is easy to watch because he's generally quiet and calm. That's partly because of his personality and partly because he's on medication, especially at night, when he gets a sedative to help him sleep. But those medications have to be administered on a strict schedule, and if even one dose is missed, his schedule is completely thrown off. That means we have to be sure our babysitters know exactly what they're doing so Jaxon doesn't miss a dose or get an overdose. The medicine isn't the only tricky part, either. After he eats, he must be burped through a burp tube—another procedure that intimidates most babysitters.

Since we're so familiar with Jaxon's needs, it's often easier to take Jaxon out with us, although he does require quite a bit of extra gear. We have a portable backpack we can put his feeding tube in. We also pack up his special positional wheelchair, which holds him upright. Then there's his diaper bag, which is filled with formula, water, medications, syringes, a pump, and a milk bag—along with the usual baby necessities like burp cloths, diapers, and wipes. We've learned to carry extra supplies in the car so we never have to worry about running out of essentials like food or medicine.

It's easy to feel guilty if we want to take some personal time to golf, shop, or watch a sporting event. When we do go out, it isn't long before we're thinking about Jaxon, picturing him at home and wondering if he needs anything.

But early on I realized we'd have to be superhuman if

we didn't need an occasional break. Getting away helps us recharge and refresh so we can pick up our responsibilities again and keep being there for Jaxon. We didn't become saints or angels when we received a child with special needs. We have to keep balanced as individuals, and we need to continue working on our marriage. Now that we've been Jaxon's parents for a while, Brittany and I are able to admit that sometimes we need a break.

When we were in the hospital after Jaxon was born, my brother-in-law, Joey, pulled me aside. By that point we'd been at the hospital every day for more than three weeks, and we believed Jaxon was about to die. Joey, who has been involved in youth and music ministry at his church for years, looked me in the eye and gave me some pointed advice: "I've watched families who have gone through situations like this," he said. "Everyone is focused on the child, as they should be. But I've seen families who concentrate so much on their child that they forget about their marriage. When their child doesn't make it, they also lose their marriage because they've grown apart." He wanted to make sure we made it a priority to stay connected.

Joey's advice has remained with me, and I'm aware that this isn't a one-time decision—it's something I need to put into action on a regular basis. Every day I try to remind myself that I'm not only working for my son; I'm also working for Brittany and our marriage. Date nights may be rare, but we appreciate them when they happen, and we're grateful for the people who help make them possible.

I know we're not alone in this struggle. When any overwhelming situation overtakes our lives, it's easy to become so focused on that one thing that we forget we're more than one-dimensional. If you lose someone you love, you may be so overcome with grief that you forget the other people who love you or assume that they no longer need you. If you have an accident or a health crisis, you may become so withdrawn and depressed over what you can no longer do that you don't realize how many opportunities still await you.

I'm not trying to downplay the pain and heartbreak of your situation or encourage you to go into denial. But as you face the realities of your circumstances, you can still be present in your life. Keep going to church or book club or dinner with your friend. Don't close yourself off from the people who love you. In time, your situation will shift, and you don't want to have shut yourself off to everything except your one defining circumstance. You need to keep living.

Thankfully, Jaxon is calmer and easier to manage these days, and our family members are more comfortable taking care of him. That means it's not just Brittany and me working to keep our marriage healthy—the entire family is on our team, and we've grown so much closer since Jaxon arrived. In a way, I guess you could say we've all become Jaxon Strong.

Until we had Jaxon, we never fully realized how important family is. And our family isn't just Brittany, Jaxon, and me—it's also our parents, siblings, and assorted uncles, aunts, and cousins.

At first I think our family felt a little helpless, especially Brittany's family, who live far away in Rhode Island

and North Carolina. We get that—after all, Brittany and I felt helpless too. But even though our family couldn't do much to help with our medical struggles, they stepped in to help out in their own unique ways. Shortly after Jaxon was born, my mom did some grocery shopping for us and my dad redeemed the hour or two I would have spent each week keeping our

Florida lawn trimmed. Every effort they have made on our behalf has helped me spend more time serving my wife and son.

With every visit, our family is excited to see Jaxon's progress. They are all comfortable with him now, and he has learned to recognize his grandparents and respond to them. Although he is limited in many ways, he knows their voices, and when he hears them, he perks up.

The other day my mom, Lynne, picked Jaxon up. "Come see Nona," she said. Jaxon responded by snuggling chest-to-chest with her—something he usually only does with Brittany. It may sound like a little thing, but that day marked a milestone in their relationship—one they'll continue to build as the days go by.

Pay it forward.

Before we had Jaxon, we never thought much about paying it forward. Now it's something Brittany and I think about all the time. We've been blessed to receive from so many people, and now we also get to experience the joy of giving. Both are equally important.

One night we met some friends for dinner in Orlando. Jaxon was with us, and while we were enjoying our dinner, we couldn't help but notice the family at the next table. A young couple sat there with two young children, a boy and a girl. The kids were adorable—but they were also lively and loud. The parents looked a little stressed out, and we knew how they felt. We understood how much time it takes to get kids ready to go out, and we also knew how important it is to do that once in a while.

Brittany and I decided to talk to the waitress and anonymously cover the family's restaurant check. The friends we were with loved the idea because they, too, could relate to what it's like to feel stressed out by lively kids, whether they have special needs or not.

It's true that we live in an increasingly uncivil world, but even so, some people still practice the art of kindness. Perhaps they have been the recipients of generosity themselves, and now they're paying it forward. The phrase "random acts of kindness" was coined by Anne Herbert in 1982, and since then the idea has taken off. In 1993, a book with that title was published promoting this thought: "Imagine what would happen if there was an outbreak of kindness in the world, if everybody did one kind thing on a daily basis." The book became an instant bestseller, spawning offshoots such as these:

- An annual Random Act of Kindness (RAOK) Week, in which participants are encouraged to pay the toll of the person on the road behind them, shovel their neighbor's driveway, or offer flowers to a coworker they usually clash with.
- RAOK clubs, which offer gifts to strangers on the

subway and deliver "baskets of joy" to nursing homes, hospitals, and rehab centers.

- An RAOK world movement, which is spreading through classrooms, churches, hospitals, businesses, websites, and service clubs.
- RAOK emphases in schools, where some principals give deserving students certificates that say "Caught you being kind."
- An endorsement from Princess Diana: "Perhaps we're too embarrassed to change or too frightened of the consequences of showing that we actually care. But why not risk it anyway? Begin today. Carry out a random act of seemingly senseless kindness, with no expectation of reward or punishment, safe in the knowledge that one day, someone somewhere might do the same for you."
- Thousands of suggestions for everyday acts of kindness, such as adopting a stray animal, smiling at the bus driver, really listening to someone, giving a stranger a sincere compliment, returning shopping carts to the store, writing a thank-you note, buying dog biscuits for your neighbor's dog, painting flowers on the envelopes you mail, treating your local police officer to coffee, or giving up your place in line at the

grocery store to the person behind you with just one item.[1]

Because people have been so generous to us, we love being generous toward others. We've found that giving is both contagious and addictive. Many times we'll go through the Chick-fil-A drive-thru and pay for the car behind us—and then we get giddy with anticipation, wondering how long the chain of giving will go on.

Giving can catch fire. Last year I heard about a customer at a Starbucks drive-thru who paid for the car behind him. The second car paid for the third, and the chain of generosity continued without pause for seven hours. Isn't that incredible? Now imagine that happening on a larger scale!

We don't believe in trumpeting the details about our giving, because Jesus said the purpose behind our giving shouldn't be to get the glory ourselves: "When you give to someone in need, don't do as the hypocrites do. . . . Don't let your left hand know what your right hand is doing. Give your gifts in private, and your Father, who sees everything, will reward you" (Matthew 6:2-4).

Yet at times it *is* good to share the news of giving. Jesus said, "No one lights a lamp and then puts it under a basket. Instead, a lamp is placed on a stand, where it gives light to everyone in the house. In the same way, let your good deeds shine out for all to see, so that everyone will praise your heavenly Father" (Matthew 5:15-16). We want to share our story of generosity to let other people know the joy that can come from both receiving and giving.

We have established a tax-deductible foundation that people can give to in order to help other children like Jaxon. The foundation's mission focuses on three specific areas: supporting neurological research, advocating for those with disabilities, and upholding the value of every life.

We are energized by the thought of helping others through an organization that bears our son's name. Jaxon: "God has been gracious and shown devotion." And Emmett: "hardworking." Brittany and I chose those names before Jax was born, but now we truly appreciate their meanings. In our opinion, no child has ever worked harder to strive for life and for each milestone than Jaxon, and God has been unspeakably gracious to us. He has given us so much that we *must* give to others in return.

Giving is contagious.

Most people know that Dave Thomas, founder of the Wendy's hamburger chain, sold hamburgers and fries and Frostys and made a lot of money doing it. But what a lot of people don't know is that Dave Thomas gave millions of dollars back to the communities that supported him.

In an interview, Thomas explained his philosophy: "Profit is not a dirty word. We all talk about achieving our dreams and accomplishing our goals. But let's not forget that making a profit gets us there. Profit in business means expansion, growth, and opportunities. It also means you can share your profit with your management team and the community. Profit means success, and success means sharing with others."[2]

Dave Thomas established the Dave Thomas Foundation for Adoption, a public nonprofit organization that promotes adoption and makes it easier for parents to adopt children. He also supported the Children's Home Society of Florida and provided the seed money to build the I. Lorraine Thomas Children's Home, a temporary emergency home for children in Fort Lauderdale. He provided generous donations to children's hospitals, including the Children's Hospital in Columbus, the Arthur G. James Cancer Hospital and Richard J. Solove Research Institute at Ohio State University, and St. Jude Children's Research Hospital in Memphis.[3]

Dave Thomas started from humble beginnings: he was a high school dropout and a former Walgreens soda jerk. But people invested in him, including the couple who adopted him when he was six weeks old, and Grandma

Minnie, who taught him the values of hard work and treating others with respect. After years of dedication and hard work, he amassed a fortune and was able to pay his blessings forward, happily giving much of it away to improve the lives of children.

Thankfully, you don't have to own a restaurant franchise to make a difference in the world. On a much smaller scale, Brittany and I have discovered what he knew: we are blessed to be a blessing. And there's a secret we've discovered about giving along the way: generosity is contagious. Try it, and you'll see.

Celebrate Everyday Victories

Brittany
Sometimes miracles come in ordinary moments.

Until Jaxon was born, I never realized how momentous and precious even the smallest milestones could be. Healthy babies progress at an astounding rate. One day your child is a helpless bundle in your arms, and a few months later, that baby is holding up his head and rolling over. At six months, healthy babies are sitting up on their own, and by about a year, they're beginning to walk and talk.

Jaxon, however, hasn't progressed at the same rate as other children his age. His brain is one-fifth of the size it should be. But although his brain is malformed and smaller than usual, you might be surprised by how much he has learned to do. One of the brain's unique attributes is its ability to adapt. Given time and training and attention, the brain can adjust—and God can work miracles.

As I write this, Jaxon is eighteen months old and can't sit up without support. He can't crawl, and he can't walk. He can't roll from his back to his tummy or vice versa. He can't hold a pencil or do his taxes yet either.

But we've stopped thinking about the milestones he hasn't reached, because we are so thrilled by the milestones he *has* reached. Just the other day I saw my tired boy rub his eye with the back of his hand—a gesture he had never made before. With his physical limitations, he shouldn't be able to do that. But he did.

Yesterday I dashed into the bathroom to apply my makeup while Jaxon sat on his beanbag chair with a turtle toy—one that lights up and plays music when you press a button on the turtle's back. The house was silent, and then I suddenly heard the music. Jax had found a way to hit the button—completely on his own!

Jaxon used to hate taking a bath, especially during his irritability phase. When we put him in the tub, he would toss his head back, stiffen, scream, and turn as red as a tomato. It took both Brandon and me to bathe him, and we were both exhausted afterward. Jaxon resisted the bath so vigorously that for a while we wondered if the water was somehow painful for him. It wasn't—he simply didn't like it. For months he would scream throughout his bath time, making it clear that he wasn't happy.

Then we came up with the idea of getting a medical

chair for him to sit in while we bathed him. This support helped Jaxon feel more comfortable and secure, and he started to enjoy his bath. Now we can't even say the word *bath* unless we're ready to head straight to the tub, because he gets so excited. Whenever he hears us talking about a bath, he immediately starts babbling as if to say, "Hello? Didn't you say something about a bath?"

The job that used to require two people now only needs one, though Brandon and I usually bathe Jaxon together because we enjoy it. Now Jaxon sits in his chair and kicks at his toys as they bob in the water. After we've washed him, we take the chair out of the tub, hold him horizontally, and let him "swim" for a few minutes. He kicks and moves his arms freely, and he complains when it's time to take him out of the water. While we're dressing him afterward, he fusses, letting us know that he'd rather be in the tub. The only way to quiet his complaining is to distract him with a book or a toy.

The other night I wanted to give Jaxon a quick bath so Brandon and I could sit and relax before we went to bed. Brandon made a trip to the grocery store, and I thought I could pop Jaxon into the tub and be done in about ten minutes. After I got the water ready and laid out his towel and washcloth, I picked Jaxon up and put him in the bath. He hadn't been in two seconds when . . . well, let's just say he polluted the water with a substance that usually ends up in a diaper.

"Jaxon!"

Not knowing what else to do, I pulled him out of the tub and took him to the sink. "No swim time tonight," I said. "Sorry, buddy." I put a towel on the rim of the sink to support his head, turned on the water, and added some soap. Then I put Jaxon in. He fit snugly, his knees tight against his chest, and for a moment he looked at me as if I'd lost my mind. Then his expression clouded—he was mad that he wasn't in the bathtub. But the longer he sat there, the more Jaxon began to enjoy this new, cozy arrangement. By the time I was ready to dry him off, he fussed at me for taking him out of the sink.

Our little boy has become a water baby.

So often we look for miracles and God's intervention in the big things—in large-scale answers to prayer. But living with Jaxon has taught us that sometimes God works in the small, seemingly ordinary things, like when a little boy learns to play with his favorite toy or when a daily chore is transformed into a delight.

Your everyday miracles may look different from ours. Maybe you've been working to restore a relationship, and healing is coming slowly, one conversation at a time. Or maybe you are battling an addiction, and it takes every ounce of effort to make the hard, right choice each day. But regardless of the challenge you're up against, know that God delights in these victories, small as they may seem. The prophet Zechariah puts it this way: "Do not despise these small beginnings, for the LORD rejoices to see the work begin" (Zechariah 4:10).

Don't get tired of doing what's good.

Whenever Jaxon accomplishes something—whether it's moving his hand, taking a step, or turning his head—we clap and shout and praise him like crazy. We tell him he's a smart boy and a strong boy—and to us, he is all of those things. He gets excited whenever he learns a new skill too, especially if he gets to watch a video of himself.

After one victory during tummy time in his room, Brandon and I were startled when he released a sound we'd never heard from him before. Thrilled by his success at turning his head to the right—opposite his muscles' inclination—he responded with a gut-busting belly laugh.

Jaxon is now able to take steps when we guide him with our hands. One deliberate step at a time, he lifts his legs and plants them on the floor, inching forward as we support him. To the amazement of everyone who predicted that Jaxon would be little more than a living lump of flesh, he has achieved milestones he was never supposed to achieve. We are confident that he will continue to progress on his own timetable.

Although Jaxon is growing more slowly than the average child—at eighteen months he weighed only twelve pounds—he continues to make progress physically. And other than three bouts with a common cold, he has never been sick. In spite of all his setbacks, he's a healthy, happy baby.

Jaxon still uses a feeding tube. The swallow reflex is tied up with chewing, and he needs therapy to get those two functions in sync with each other. But every once in a while we'll give him a tiny bit of avocado or baby cookies to put in his mouth. The baby cookies dissolve in his mouth, and he likes them so much he'll eat an entire cookie in one sitting. His little taste buds work great, and he's quick to let us know when he doesn't like a particular taste. He'll shiver, make a face, and spit out the offending substance. We love his emotional reactions, because they demonstrate his personality and his distinct preferences.

He eats slowly, at his own pace, but he enjoys it. Jaxon's

way of eating—slow and steady—is a metaphor for his progress. It's slow and steady and miraculous.

During the Super Bowl game when Jaxon was about seventeen months old, I was sitting on the couch with him, trying to get interested in the game. I'm not a huge football fan, but our family was over and everyone was having fun watching the game together. Jax, who was in my lap, was trying to chew on my finger when a thought struck me. *Maybe he's ready for the pacifier!*

When Jaxon was first born, the nurses tried to get him to take a pacifier in the hospital, but he wanted nothing to do with it. He would play around with it, lick it, and spit it out. He would hold it in his mouth for only a few seconds. That was when we realized he wouldn't be able to eat on his own—he hadn't developed the natural suck-swallow reflex.

After bringing Jaxon home, we tried to get him to take a pacifier several times. We knew that pacifiers do more than soothe fussy babies. It's important for babies to learn to suck, because the more they use their mouth muscles, the sooner they'll be able to eat on their own. We tried various shapes of pacifiers, different brands, and even bottle nipples with milk in them, but Jaxon just wasn't able to hold any of them in his mouth. He couldn't breathe and suck at the same time.

But on Super Bowl Sunday, I thought maybe the time

had come. I found a pacifier and settled back on the couch, slipping it into Jaxon's mouth. It took about ten minutes for him to realize what was happening, but eventually he latched on and began to suck. I was so excited that I grabbed my phone to record a video for the Jaxon Strong Facebook page. We were making progress!

Since then we've given Jaxon the pacifier many times. He'll take it and suck for about half an hour before spitting it out. His muscles have developed enough that he is able to take it any time he wants.

I believe that one of the reasons Jaxon is making such significant progress is because of all the time we spend with him. Every morning we play with him. By the time the sun sets, we've said "I love you" dozens of times. We call him by his name so he'll recognize it. We say things like "Mommy loves you!" "Daddy loves you!" "We love you so much!" "We're so proud of you." "You're a strong boy!" "You're so smart." He hears positive words from us every day because we believe that this positive reinforcement is having an amazing effect on his progress.

And it's not just Jaxon who is benefiting: he's making a difference in the lives of others, too. We've heard from people from all faith backgrounds and all walks of life who have been encouraged by Jaxon's journey and accomplishments.

So are we.

What have you celebrated lately? Losing a pound or two? Making it through the day without a cigarette? Resisting the urge to check your phone at the family dinner table? Sometimes we grow immune to the ordinary wonders of life—to all the victories, large and small, that are being won by the people around us. Your coworkers, your neighbors, the people who sit near you at church—they are fighting battles too. There are parents struggling to gain wisdom as their children go through the turbulent teen years. There are single parents who are exhausting themselves, trying to be everything their kids need them to be.

Maybe these small steps toward victory don't seem like much, and you feel discouraged. Maybe you wonder if your battle is lost.

Let me assure you: it's not. As long as you're alive, you're not finished, and neither are the people you love. So lift your head, take a deep breath, and catch your second wind. Confide your struggles to a trusted friend, and listen to them cheer you on as you return to the fray.

Just as Jaxon works to grow his underdeveloped muscles, you, too, can get stronger and forge ahead. "So let's not get tired of doing what is good," the apostle Paul writes. "At just the right time we will reap a harvest of blessing if we don't give up" (Galatians 6:9).

Hang in there! And when you or your loved ones win a victory, no matter how small it seems, celebrate it!

∽

Brandon

Some heroes come in small packages.

Recently I heard a story about one of the great presidents of Harvard University, Charles William Eliot. Born with a serious facial disfigurement, Eliot discovered as a young man that nothing could be done about it. He would have to go through life with this horrible mark. When his mother relayed that tragic truth to him, it was "the dark hour of his soul."

His mother said, "My son, it is not possible for you to get rid of this handicap. We have consulted the best surgeons, and they say that nothing can be done. But it is possible for you, with God's help, to grow a mind and soul so big that people will forget to look at your face."[1]

Until we had Jaxon, I never realized the tremendous strength and resilience of the human spirit—even within a tiny child.

As a kid, I always admired professional athletes. I appreciated the level of excellence a player had to achieve to make it to the big leagues—the skill, determination, perseverance, courage, and sacrifice of time and energy.

I especially admired Cal Ripken Jr., the "Iron Man" of baseball, who holds the record for the most consecutive games ever played. Ripken, who could have been sidelined as a result of injuries, illness, or sloppy play, played 2,632 consecutive games over his sixteen-plus seasons in professional baseball. This broke the previous record held by Lou Gehrig, which had stood for fifty-six years. Ripken's feat is unlikely to be repeated, as few athletes play more than a few hundred consecutive games before succumbing to illness or injury.

These days I find myself admiring someone else who has risen above the experts' expectations: my son. Watching my favorite sports teams brings me a lot of joy, but nothing compares to watching Jaxon accomplish something he has worked hard to achieve. And while athletes gain a lot of attention for doing the things they've trained to do, Jaxon gets a lot of praise for doing things he *shouldn't* be able to do. Yes, he thrives on our encouragement, but it's also obvious he has an inner drive to make progress.

Jaxon's victories may seem small in other people's eyes, but when he takes a step or stretches out his hand or makes a new sound, the three of us feel as though he's just run an entire marathon. It's a major victory for him—and for us. When he reaches for a toy or he looks at us and laughs in response to something we've said or done, I'm reminded once again that a pint-sized boy is my hero.

In order to be a hero, you don't have to be the biggest or the strongest or the best. You just have to show up and take one small step at a time toward victory.

Mind Your Words

Brandon

Redefine the value of a human life.

Thanks to Jaxon, we are now more aware of the power of language. We have come to realize that there is a vast difference between referring to our son as a "special-needs child" and "a child with special needs."

I learned this lesson from the mother of a child with special needs. I had written something in a Facebook post about Jaxon being a "special-needs child," and she gently corrected me. I saw her point at once. Jaxon is not a substandard version of a human child. He is a valuable human being who happens to have a medical condition that requires special treatment.

Though I am occasionally tempted to refer to a "special-needs child" in an effort to avoid a mouthful of words, I'm aware that in choosing that shortcut, I'm settling for an inferior descriptor. Jaxon and other children like him will always be children first, not a bundle of "special needs."

People have a tendency to identify others by their most noticeable trait—"the pretty one," "the heavy girl," "the

Asian kid," "the goofy one." It might just seem like short-hand, but it's really not fair, because people are so much more than a single trait. The pretty girl might be a genius, and the goofy boy might be the world's greatest inventor . . . but no one knows it yet. I've been trying to stop using these verbal shortcuts to identify people—I'd much prefer to use a person's name.

Language has the power to influence people in such subtle ways that we need to be aware of the words we use. An adoptive parent once told me that the adoption community has special sensitivities as well. Adoptive parents never refer to biological children as "natural" or "our own" because *all* their children are their own—and none of them are artificial. Biological parents don't "give their children away"; they make adoption plans for their children.

Perhaps one of the most obvious ways our culture participates in a subtle war of words is in the conversation about abortion. The word itself is so loaded with negative connotations that abortion advocates call themselves "pro-choice" while those who disagree with the ethics of abortion are "pro-life." Abortion providers speak of "the fetus" while abortion opponents always speak of "the baby." Patients who visit an abortion clinic are there for "termination," not to have their unborn babies killed and removed from the womb. More than one million babies are aborted each year in the United States, and this dehumanizing language obscures that awful truth. When we believe that a human life has value and dignity from conception, that truth should be reflected in the way we speak.

Words are powerful—and we often use them to trick our minds into accepting situations we could not otherwise tolerate. As the Allies closed in on the Axis powers near the end of World War II, the Nazis intended to burn the dead and eradicate all traces of the mass graves in Vilna. A Jewish man who was ordered to help open one of the mass graves later reported, "When we first opened the graves, we couldn't help it, we all burst out sobbing. . . . The Germans even forbade us to use the words 'corpse' or 'victim.' The dead were blocks of wood . . . with absolutely no importance. . . . The Germans made us refer to the bodies as *Figuren*, that is, as puppets, as dolls, or as *Schmattes*, which means 'rags.' . . . The head of the Vilna Gestapo told us: 'There are ninety thousand people lying there, and absolutely no trace must be left of them.'"[1]

Knowing that humans are made in the image of God with eternal souls as well as physical bodies, we ought to respect and treasure each human life. But as our society continues its shift toward secularism, where we ignore not only God but also His eternal truths, we tend to focus on "quality of life" as though that alone were the basis of human worth.

In a court case a number of years ago, a motorcycle accident victim who had been paralyzed from the neck down wanted to have his ventilator removed—an act that would result in his death. Because officials at the nursing home where he was a patient would not remove his life support, he sued, and the judge ruled in his favor. The judge said, "The ventilator to which he is attached is not prolonging his life; it is prolonging his death."[2]

Joni Eareckson Tada, founder and CEO of Joni and Friends International Disability Center, offered this response: "That [ruling] made me, an activist and advocate, steaming mad! If that judge had been approached by a poor minority woman who could no longer endure racism, sexism, and poverty, and she wanted aid to end her life painlessly, the woman would have been refused flat-out. In fact, she would be offered support in seeking better housing and a job, and placed in a suicide-prevention program. But when a disabled person . . . declares the same intention, people assume he is acting rationally."[3]

People who feel that they lack a certain quality of life ought to seek help for their *lives*, not their deaths. Brittany and I are seeking every possible avenue of help for Jaxon—we would do anything to improve his life. What parent wouldn't do the same for a much-loved child?

Author Karl Barth warned that the value of a human life is not always discernible to the human eye:

A man who is not, or is no longer, capable of work, of earning, of enjoyment and even perhaps of communication, is not for this reason unfit to live, least of all because he cannot render to the existence of the state any notable or active contribution, but can only directly or indirectly become a burden to it. The value of this kind of life is God's secret. Those around and society as a whole may not find anything in it, but this does not mean that they have a right to reject and liquidate it. Who can really see the true and inward reality of this type of life? Who can really know whether it may not be far more precious in the eyes of God, or reveal itself as far more glorious in eternity, than the lives of hundreds of healthy workers and peasants, technicians, scientists, artists and soldiers, which the state rates so highly? . . . No community, whether family, village or state, is really strong if it will not carry its weak and even its very weakest members. They belong to it no less than the strong, and the quiet work of their maintenance and care, which might seem useless on a superficial view, is perhaps far more effective than common labor, culture or historical conflict in knitting it closely and securely together. On the other hand, a community which regards and treats its weak members as a hindrance, and even proceeds to their extermination, is on the verge of collapse. The killing of the weak for the sake of others hampered by their weakness can rest only on a misconception of the life which in its specific form, and therefore even in its weakness, is always given by God and should therefore be an object of respect to others.[4]

A friend of ours told us about a woman named Hazel, who had been severely crippled by rheumatoid arthritis. Near the end of her life, Hazel was bedridden and was being cared for by family members. She was no longer able to do the volunteer work she had once enjoyed. To a disinterested outsider, Hazel might have seemed useless.

But Hazel's family loved her. They tenderly cared for her, growing in the virtues of love and patience as they bathed her, fed her, and turned her in her bed. They shared laughs and reminisced over favorite family memories.

And despite what an outside observer might have assumed, Hazel was *not* unproductive. As she lay in bed, she prayed for her family, her church, and her friends. She asked God to take care of her pastor, her neighbors, and the president. She prayed for her nation, for the lost and the hurting around the world, and for missionaries who risked their lives to share God's love with others.

How many of those people knew that Hazel was praying for them, often by name? How many of them knew that her voice, frail as it was, brought their requests to God's ears? How many of them realized that Hazel shed compassionate tears for them—for their health, their needs, and their salvation?

We can't judge the productivity of any life, because we don't know what happens in that intimate place between a soul and God. Nor should we attempt to measure the worth of any life, because God loved the entire world so much—He valued every life so highly—that He sent His Son to die for us.

Occasionally Brittany and I read comments online responding to videos or articles about Jaxon's story. I've been amazed and shocked by the cruelty of some of those comments. Many of them are unprintable, and I wouldn't want to repeat them anyway. Others have been unbelievably harsh, urging us to "kill that kid" or accusing us of using him for money and fame. Others call us heartless and cruel because we didn't terminate Jaxon's life before he was born.

These comments make me want to weep for the state of our culture. Only fifty years ago, before abortion was legal, no one would have suggested that we kill our son before his birth. If Jaxon had been born then, he would have entered a world that didn't have the technological advances we have today, and it would have been more of a struggle to make sure he was comfortable, content, and healthy. Because he weighed only four pounds at birth, he might not have survived even if he'd been born with a complete brain. But modern medicine routinely saves small babies today, and never has a child with unique challenges enjoyed a greater chance of survival.

As for those who claim that Jaxon has no quality of life, no consciousness, no way to feel happiness or joy or love . . . well, they haven't spent time with our son. They haven't watched him smile when we greet him in the morning or seen him smack his lips on his mommy's nose in an effort to return her kisses. They haven't heard him belly laugh or seen him exert every ounce of his energy to get his turtle toy to play music. They haven't seen him focus on a shining light and smile at it.

They don't know anything about the quality of his life, but we do. And because he is God's gift to us, we will love him every day that God allows him to remain with us.

Ignore the naysayers.

Since Jaxon's birth, Brittany and I continue to be surprised by how many people have strong opinions about how we should raise him or what decisions should be made on his behalf. I'm always baffled when I hear from people who have never met Jaxon but assume they know how he thinks, acts, and feels. Even though they don't have medical training, they think they are a good judge of whether his actions are voluntary or involuntary. Some people assume that he is in constant pain and that we are selfish parents for not allowing him to die shortly after birth.

When we first learned about Jaxon's condition, we knew we'd have only one opportunity to do everything we could for him. We had been given a child, and it was our duty to give him the best chance possible. I have never understood how choosing to give Jaxon a chance at survival could be considered selfish. How is killing him better than fighting for him to live? Since when did choosing life become selfish?

If we had terminated the pregnancy, the world would never have heard of Jaxon Strong. The thousands of people who have been inspired and encouraged by his determination would never have heard of the little boy who courageously fights for each milestone on a daily basis. The parents who have received the news that they have a child with a similar condition would not know that it's possible for a child to survive with microhydran-encephaly.

As for us, if we had terminated Brittany's pregnancy, we would have spent the rest of our lives wondering if the doctors had diagnosed him correctly—when, in fact, they had not. We would have looked at our empty nursery and wondered what our son would have been like. We never would have held Jaxon in our arms, smiled into his big blue eyes, or heard him call for us.

Yes, we've shed tears over our son and the challenges he faces. But we've also wept tears of joy, and we've given him more kisses than we can count. We have given him love, and he has given love right back. When he snuggles against my chest or gives Brittany a slobbery kiss, he affirms our decision to give him life and to love him. Even if he couldn't do anything to show us love in return, we would still love him—because he's our son, and he's precious in the sight of God.

In *Ethics for a Brave New World*, the authors write about the importance of choosing life for unborn babies with potentially life-threatening conditions:

A commonly heard argument for abortion is that we should not allow "nature's anomalies" to be born. Where possible, we ought to abort children who will be born with some handicap, particularly if it is severe.

In response, we have a number of things to say. First, society in general and family and friends in particular must deal compassionately with any parent called upon to take up the added burden of caring for a handicapped child. Even when that burden is accepted, it is not easy. It often requires enormous sacrifice. . . .

Second, it is easy to forget that there are at least two parties to be considered in this matter, the parents and the handicapped child. It is important not to pit the parents' needs against the child's. Put another way, the child's right to life should not be bartered for freedom from care for the parents. It is hard to imagine a parent asking God for a handicapped child. However, many testify that just such a child has been an incredible blessing, even drawing the family closer together and to the Lord. We should not forget Christ's attitude toward those who were sick and infirm (e.g., John 9:3). . . .

Third, handicaps cover a wide range of

disabilities. Some children are born with mild handicaps, others with moderate, and still others with severe disabilities. To summarily condemn them all as a group to death is cruel indeed. . . . The desire to cure or avoid disease should not so consume us that we destroy those among us who have disabilities. A utopian society is a tricky one. It immediately raises the question, whose utopia? One must be careful not to ticket oneself for termination in the process.[5]

Someone once criticized Brittany and me, saying that Jaxon's life was "wasting tax dollars" because of his medical needs. The implication was that the wiser economical option would be to terminate our son's life. That leads to some significant follow-up questions: What about the child who was born "normal" but is later diagnosed with cancer? Should his parents be ashamed for giving their child life or for fighting for his life after his diagnosis? Should elderly patients with dementia surrender their lives when their intellect begins to decline?

We are all part of the human community, created by God. He has commissioned us to support, defend, and comfort one another. Those who battle adversity, whether physical or mental challenges, should be affirmed and valued as fully human individuals who can also be sources of inspiration and examples of courage. Life is precious, and it should always be valued.

At the time of Jaxon's diagnosis, it seemed like micro-hydranencephaly was a death sentence. But we have since learned that some patients have lived into their thirties, enjoying relatively normal lives and developing the use of their senses. Yes, they experience struggles and limitations, but they also recognize their families and find ways to communicate. Jaxon is certainly on the right path, and we believe God isn't finished with him yet.

On January 22, 2016, the forty-third anniversary of the *Roe v. Wade* Supreme Court decision, I was invited to tell Jaxon's story at a March for Life rally in Washington, DC. I got choked up during that public speech—my first—but I was grateful for the opportunity to tell the world about Jaxon. The main message I wanted to get across was how much Brittany and I love our little boy and how we marvel at the miracle he is. In a room filled with politicians, pro-life advocates, and members of the media, I watched men and women flush with emotion as I spoke of our love for our son. Later, one of the organizers told me that by the time I'd finished, there wasn't a dry eye in the room.

Our precious son sleeps in a crib near our bed. The last thing I do every night is lean over the edge of the crib, kiss him, and say, "I love you, Jaxon." And the first thing I do every morning is go to his bed, check to be sure he's still breathing, and kiss him again.

I treasure my son. Loving him has brought incredible joy and depth to my life. So what do I feel toward those who don't understand that?

I feel sorry for them.

❧

Brittany
Focus on the good.
Because positive words have the power to bless someone's life, we speak positively about Jaxon whenever we can and stay focused on the good. We also try our best to remember to express our gratitude.

I love this quote by G. K. Chesterton:

You say grace before meals.
All right.
But I say grace before the play and the opera,
And grace before the concert and the pantomime,
And grace before I open a book,
And grace before sketching, . . . boxing, walking,
*   playing, dancing;*
And grace before I dip the pen in the ink.[6]

Brandon and I give thanks for pacifiers, MIC-KEY buttons, and toys that light up when touched. We give thanks for every bit of baby babble. We are grateful for every one of Jaxon's smiles. When we thank God for these things, we're reminded that we aren't doing this on our own. We have supernatural support.

We are grateful for the ways our lives have been changed by our son. We have learned to be kinder to each other, to our neighbors, and to strangers. We have learned that every child is precious and that every life is sacred. We have discovered that God doesn't make mistakes, so every situation that isn't "normal" is something He allowed. The part that's up to us is how we as humans will handle it.

Will we allow our child to ridicule the student at school who walks with an obvious limp? Will we avoid speaking to the new neighbor who is a different race or culture? Will we stare through the homeless man on the street corner?

Our heavenly Father has given us power over our tongues—over what we choose to say and not say. We can use our words to build others up or tear them down. At the end of his letter to the Corinthians, the apostle Paul gives these instructions: "Be joyful. Grow to maturity. Encourage each other. Live in harmony and peace. Then the God of love and peace will be with you" (2 Corinthians

13:11). Although these words were written thousands of years ago, they are still relevant today.

Our words matter—they have the power to tear down or to build up. Use your words to bring life!

Slow Down

Brittany

Savor the little things.

One of the gifts Jaxon has given us is a new perspective on how precious and fleeting life is. His little life has shown us the importance of investing our time wisely and intentionally. Thanks to our son, we now know in a very real way the significance of carpe diem—of not missing the important moments.

I'm reminded of this quote about the gift of time by Robert G. Lee:

> If you had a bank that credited your account each morning with $86,400, that carried no balance from day to day, allowed you to keep no cash in your account, and finally every evening canceled whatever part of the amount you had failed to use during the day, what would you do? Draw out every cent—of course! Well, you have such a bank and its name is "Time." Every morning it credits you with 86,400 seconds. Every night it rules

off—as lost—whatever of this you have failed to invest to good purpose. It carries no balances. It allows no balances. It allows no overdrafts. Each day the bank named "Time" opens a new account with you. Each night it burns the records of the day. If you fail to use the day's deposits, the loss is yours.[1]

Brandon and I both used to have full-time jobs. We used to schedule virtually every free minute. We'd come home, work out, and then eat dinner. On weekends we often ran 5Ks. We loved having a full schedule, and we didn't understand couples who veg in front of the TV. We were constantly busy—always going, going, going. If by chance we found ourselves at home with nothing to do, I'd say, "Let's go do something," and we'd head out the door.

Things changed when Jaxon arrived. Now we stay home a lot, and we love it. There's nothing I enjoy more than holding Jaxon on my lap and reading a book to him. He loves Dr. Seuss, and his eyes get as big as dinner plates when I turn those colorful pages and let him enjoy the rhythm of the words.

When Jaxon was in his fussy stage, he'd go from screaming to quiet when I began to read to him. Some people might question why we'd read books to our son when he will probably never read himself, but we believe he's learning in his own way—and besides, we all love this bonding time!

I see it as a privilege to be Jaxon's mommy and to spend lots of time with him. More than ever, I'm seeing that earthly time is a finite thing, and all of us only have so much to spend. Neither Jaxon nor I will live forever, and I want to make the most of the time we have.

It isn't always easy to seize each moment, however, because there are constantly less important things that clamor for our attention. For instance, we are grateful for all the support we've gotten from the media and the online community on Jaxon's behalf, but we also know we need to be careful with this attention. We never want to lose sight of the fact that Jaxon is our *son*, not our cause. His story may open doors for us to spread the word about pediatric neurological disorders, but we must never forget that we are his parents, not his promoters.

If I allow myself to be so caught up in the publicity around Jaxon that I'm not spending time with my family, then I will be the worst sort of hypocrite. Loving Jaxon means spending time with him. Loving Brandon means sharing the job of caring for our son. It means cherishing who he is apart from being Jaxon's father.

Spending quality time with Jaxon means I must meet

him on his level. There are times I need to put away all thoughts of my to-do list and do something he enjoys. It takes effort to intentionally interact with him and focus my attention completely on him, but the payoff is worth it. In those moments, it's like we're carrying on a conversation only the two of us can understand. Of course, there's also a place for sitting on the couch watching a movie with him in my arms—that's togetherness, and he knows I'm with him.

A friend once told us a story about her son, who was three at the time. He was jabbering away about something, and she was looking at her phone, scrolling through her messages. Finally her son said, "Mommy, you're not listening!"

"Yes, I am."

"No, Mommy," her son replied. "Listen to me with your *face*!"

"Face listening" is what really counts, isn't it? Whether it's our children, our spouses, our neighbors, or our friends, we need to listen with our faces and our hearts as well as our ears.

As a couple, Brandon and I are no longer reluctant to sit still. Our schedules are completely focused around family time, Jaxon's bath, and tummy time—when we play with him. We wake up and ask each other, "What can we do to make today special for Jaxon?" We've gone from being needlessly busy to making every moment count for Jaxon.

I remember seeing a commercial for charcoal once—I think it was Kingsford. The tagline was "Slow down and grill." When you're grilling, you have to wait for the flames to die down and the coals to become hot enough for you to cook without charring your food.

We happen to love grilling now. We'll take Jaxon outside with us, and once we get the grill lit, we'll sit and talk to him while the coals smolder and begin to develop a dusty coat of ash. Our son will look up at the sky and unwind; we'll listen to music and smile as his big blue eyes take in the big world around him. It's a magical time for all of us.

Brandon and I have learned to slow down together. One of our favorite pastimes is just to sit in our lawn chairs in the backyard. It's not a far-flung beach or a tourist destination, but it is ours. We love being out in the sunshine as we cherish quiet moments together.

Our priorities are much more focused now, and we don't waste our time on activities that don't line up with what's most important to us. We'd rather spend our time on things that might have an eternal impact. We spend time with our family, with friends from church, and with people who see the value in helping others.

There's a concept in Italian known as *la dolce far niente*, or "the sweetness of doing nothing." The value of "nothing," of course, is open to interpretation, because our time playing with Jaxon, enjoying our backyard, or snuggling with our baby on a Saturday afternoon is certainly not "nothing" to us. And we know it's not "nothing" to Jaxon. But doing nothing certainly can be sweet!

We don't know if we'll have Jaxon next year . . . nor do we know if we'll have each other. But as long as God allows us to be a family, we're going to seize and cherish each moment.

We don't want to miss a thing.

∾

Brandon
Practice patience.

Before Jaxon came into our lives, Brittany and I didn't realize how unimportant daily frustrations are. Things like driving behind a slow driver or standing in a long grocery line used to drive me crazy. But now if I see someone in the line ahead of me struggling to find the correct change, I'm more likely to reach into my pocket to help out than to grumble. I know how it feels to struggle in public, and we've spent so much time patiently urging Jaxon to reach for his turtle or bang his toy drum that standing in a grocery line just isn't a big deal anymore.

Brittany and I used to make sure we cleaned the house every Saturday before we went out to do something fun. Now we rarely worry about whether the house is clean. We clean it when we can, and sometimes people come in to help us with vacuuming and other housework, but we no longer care if the house would pass a white-glove inspection. Jaxon is what counts, and as long as he has a safe and clean-enough environment, we figure we're doing okay. Brittany does an amazing job caring for our home, and if a few toys linger on the couch or the floor, who cares?

Life is too short to sweat the small stuff.

The other day Brittany and I were sitting on the floor in Jaxon's room, ready for tummy time with our baby. We were talking to him, coaching him, and urging him to turn his head to the right. That's a challenge for Jaxon because he has muscle spasms and a slight tic that cause his head to turn to the left. We sat there for ten minutes, clapping for Jaxon's attention, urging him on, and calling his name. Finally he turned his head to the right, and we celebrated with shouting, clapping, and lots of kisses and praise.

A child who doesn't deal with Jaxon's challenges can turn his head without thinking; Jaxon has to work at it. But during that session, Brittany and I didn't once think that Jaxon was taking too long. He's his own person, and that means he's going to learn and develop at his own pace. This is just part of his journey, and there's no need to try to rush him.

We know that throughout Jaxon's life, we will have to be patient. He won't walk at the same age as other children. He may not be able to use a toilet at two or three, when most kids start potty training. He may be ten when he masters those skills, if he masters them at all. We have to cling to hope and keep praying that Jaxon will advance as God wants him to advance, and our job is to encourage Jaxon to keep honing his skills.

In her article "The Art of Bearing Burdens," Diane Langberg writes:

> You cannot know another's experience without an investment of time. Time is a precious commodity and most of us feel we have little enough to give anywhere. However, you cannot shoulder another's burden with them without a time commitment. I will have to be willing to give you some of my time if I am to walk with you and carry a load with you. It also means that the time I give to you is largely time to be used at *your* pace. If you are carrying a burden and I come alongside to help, I will be

a hindrance if I am proceeding at twice the pace. How hard it is for us to allow another to determine our pace. How hard it is to wait while they struggle to articulate what the problem is. It is hard to wait for them to be able to hear things we think are important to say, and it is hard to manifest the patience and faithfulness of God when another's pace is about one-quarter of ours.[2]

Patience requires the sacrifice of your time—a healthy selection of sixty-second slices of your life. Exhibiting patience requires that you give something that can never be returned. It is, in short, a gift of love to your child, your spouse, or a stranger.

We are patient with Jaxon because we love him, but exhibiting patience with him has resulted in an unexpected side effect—we're beginning to be patient with other people, too. I'm learning to be patient at stoplights when the driver in front of me doesn't move after the light turns green. Every day presents a half-dozen opportunities for me to practice patience.

Brittany has an advantage—she is naturally more patient and calm than I am. "Why let other people affect your mood?" she always says. "Don't let that person rob your joy and ruin your day."

I grew up playing baseball and other competitive sports, so I'm accustomed to setting goals and working hard to achieve them. (After all, I won my wife, and that is a pretty amazing accomplishment!) But all the accomplishments in my life, in athletics or my career, pale next to that afternoon when we were working with Jaxon and he turned his head to look at us. That was one of the proudest moments of my life. When we heard him belly laugh for the first time, we were as delighted as he was. He looked like he had quills of happiness sticking out all over him—plus he knew we were thrilled and proud of him. Who can say what sort of impact that experience had on his developing mind?

Patience is extremely important when it comes to Jaxon's physical and occupational therapy. His muscles are tight, and therapy loosens them up so he can move more easily. The goal of occupational therapy is to desensitize the palms of his hands to various textures and help him acclimate to loud noises so he won't experience so many startle seizures. During tummy time, we encourage him to bear weight on his arms and reach for objects.

Jaxon disliked therapy at first, but then again, don't we all resist change? He would lift both arms and squawk, his head moving back and forth in protest. We knew this was a genuine temper tantrum, Jaxon style. But after several months, he began enjoying his therapy, and he's starting to enjoy playing with toys, too. These seem like little things, but the fact that he has worked so hard to accomplish them makes us appreciate them all the more.

Kenny Chesney has a song called "Don't Blink." If you've listened to the lyrics or seen the video, you know the song is about a younger man who is interviewing an older man, asking for advice about life. The old man gives him two words: "Don't blink." Because life rushes by faster than you'll realize, and no matter how long you think it's taking for your children to grow up or for retirement age to arrive, when you reach the winter of your life, you will look back and realize that life is like water trickling through your hands. Once a moment has passed, it can never be captured again. We have one opportunity to live each of the moments we've been given, and once they're gone, they're gone forever.

So let's do our best to make sure they've been spent for *good*.

&

Brittany
Capture the moments.
It's a common joke that young parents have albums filled with images of their first child, a single book with pictures

of their second, and almost no pictures of any children who come after that.

We take pictures and video of Jaxon almost every day—not just for us, but because we want to share his progress with all the people who are following his story through Facebook. They appreciate a little window into our world, and these glimpses allow them to witness the tremendous progress he's making as the days go by. We're grateful for pictures because they help us to slow down and remember.

Recently a photographer friend warned us that we need to print some of those images. "Paper can last for 250 years," she said, "but digital images will be around only as long as the technology to read them is. Plus, files can easily be lost or corrupted."

I'd learned that lesson the hard way only a few days earlier. My family had come over, and our niece, who's two months younger than Jaxon, loves playing with cell phones. I let her play with my phone, but I set a password on it before I handed it over. I didn't think she'd be able to hurt anything.

When I got my phone back, I was horrified to discover that she had somehow managed to program my phone back to the factory default settings. I don't know how she managed it, and I tried not to make a big deal out of it while my family was present, but once they left I picked up my phone and frantically searched for my photos. Sure enough, our photos and videos from the past year were gone! Just like that, in a digital instant, they had been wiped clean. I practically cried myself to sleep that night, thinking about the loss of so many precious moments.

Fortunately, I had sent a few of the videos and pictures to Brandon, so I was able to retrieve some of them from his phone. But I was heartbroken to lose so many memories of Jaxon, knowing he would never look exactly as he had on a particular day.

The night after I lost all my photos, we went out to dinner with Jaxon and ran into a woman who works as an associate at Target. She told me she had pictures for me. It turned out that the photo lab had messed them up, so they'd reprinted them. I could pick them up any time. "And no charge," she said, smiling.

I smiled too. After we'd lost so many other photos, her news was an unexpected and much-appreciated blessing.

We've also found that the moments don't have to be perfect to be recorded. Don't wait for that elusive window of perfection, when your whole family has coordinating outfits and everyone's hair is combed and no one is making a goofy face. Just capture life in all its ordinariness and messiness—someday those simple, everyday memories are the ones you'll appreciate the most.

We love Jaxon just the way he is, and we're not embarrassed that he doesn't look exactly like other children. We want to capture as much of his life as possible on camera. That's one reason we are so thankful for an organization called Now I Lay Me Down to Sleep, a group of professional photographers who volunteer their time and skills to go to hospitals and take photographs of babies who are stillborn or may not survive long after birth. Too many of these babies are never photographed, and many of their families would treasure a picture of their child to capture their memories. You can learn more about the organization at their website, http://www.NowILayMeDownToSleep.org.

Our memories can grow fuzzy as time passes, but photographs crystallize our memories and secure them forever. A friend of mine likes to say that we have photographs so we can have roses in December.

So slow down. Take pictures. Print them.

And remember.

Expect Miracles

Brandon

There is always hope.

Brittany and I are still in awe of the way one little baby has stirred so many people to love and compassion. Since the launch of the Jaxon Strong Facebook page, we've heard from thousands of people expressing their love and support for Jaxon. He has already touched more lives in more places than Brittany and I ever will.

Before Jaxon was born, we expected our family to love him and to support us. We weren't surprised when our friends and neighbors rallied around us with offers to help in various ways. But we have been astounded by the outpouring of love and affection from around the globe.

We've even received a couple of messages from people in the medical field. A gynecologist from another state wrote, "When we come across an ultrasound like yours, we are trained to suggest termination. But because of your son, I will stop doing that." Brittany and I could have talked for hours and not convinced this doctor to change her methods. But our son—just by being who he is—sparked a change in her heart.

Another online follower of Jaxon's—a medical staff employee—wrote, "I want you to know that one of our patients is going through a similar situation, and she has been devastated by the news. I shared the story of your son with her, and for the first time in a long while, I saw her smile."

While we know that not every baby with a brain disorder will survive for an extended time after birth, Jaxon's story has spurred many parents not to terminate their pregnancies. They have carried those babies, held them, and loved them for days or hours—whatever time they were given. And those precious moments will always be part of their family's history. Sometimes the miracle comes in the form of a supernatural healing, but other times it comes in the change that happens within us.

One of Jaxon's most generous and frequent supporters is a man who is an atheist. We have differing opinions on many important topics, but those differences don't stand in the way of our respect for one another—and his concern for Jaxon. Our lives have been enriched because Jaxon's story touched this supporter's heart.

Of all that has come out of Jaxon's story so far, we are most thrilled by messages from people who tell us that he has given them hope in their own trials and circumstances.

There is always a chance; there's a purpose in everything, even when we can't see it yet. Every day Jaxon wakes up and takes a breath, he gives hope to families in similar situations to ours—and to anyone who is struggling to overcome the odds.

Here is just a small sampling of the positive messages we receive every time we post an update on Jaxon's progress:

DS: That baby couldn't be any sweeter! You guys rock. I'm a mom of an adult child with special needs, and I know what it's like to have doctors give up on your child. Sure, my son has issues, but God's glory is displayed through him.

CR: I can't tell you how much precious Jaxon has encouraged me, just seeing how much you love him and how God is working in your lives. His beautiful eyes and curly hair, his smile and chatter and personality are all so special to see. Give him a hug and kiss from me, please!

KR: Jaxon has definitely changed my reaction to people with challenges. Because of Jaxon, I am a kinder human being. I want this little boy to succeed so bad.

DB: The whole world loves him—he's an inspiration. Considering what's going on in the world at the moment, he's a breath of fresh air, and he brings a great big smile amid the heartache and tears. XO

LM: I'm a grown man, and this fella brings me to my knees and to tears every time I see pictures of him. And I struggle for what? I want one-tenth of Jaxon's strength. God bless you, Jaxon, and your parents, too!

Not everyone is positive, of course. Occasionally we hear from people who insist that microhydranencephaly is a fatal condition and that our son can't hear, see, feel, or experience emotions. Then we look over at our boy, who is making an impact on his world every day. And those folks think *we're* the delusional ones . . .

We just smile and carry on.

∞

Brittany
Allow yourself to be surprised.
Something we learned about Jaxon early on is that music has the power to reach him in a way nothing else can.

Before Jaxon, we liked music well enough, but neither of us is especially musically inclined, and it just wasn't something we were focused on. But Brandon and I quickly noticed that music awakened something within our son, so ever since he was little, we've been playing music in the house several hours a day.

One night not long after Jaxon's birth, when we were in the NICU at the hospital, Brandon was holding Jaxon. Our baby was fussing, and nothing Brandon did could calm him. Then Brandon started singing, "No, Jaxon, no cry"—a riff on Bob Marley's "No Woman, No Cry." I was amazed when Jaxon calmed down right away.

Now I sing to Jaxon every day. I love to sing "Jesus Loves My Little Jaxon" to the tune of "Jesus Loves the Little Children." Sometimes I sing "Dancing with Mommy" as I move through the house with him in my arms, and he melts into a little love-puddle against my chest.

Jaxon first started sleeping through the night when we bought a sound machine. We set the machine on the ocean sound, and that gentle rhythm put him to sleep right away. His current sound machine plays cradle music while a projector casts images onto the ceiling—everything from a jungle scene to an ocean full of fish to the moon and stars. One time I woke up at three in the morning and heard Jaxon babbling. When I checked on him, I found him looking at the lights on the ceiling. His eyes were round and bright, and he was doing his own version of "talking"—using different syllables and pitches.

Now we're excited about the prospect of trying music therapy to help Jaxon. There's a growing body of medical research about the power of music, and many hospitals have hired music therapists to help patients with conditions ranging from autism to Alzheimer's disease. Music has also been used to treat PTSD, brain damage, chronic pain, and other conditions.[1]

On the second day of Jaxon's life—when the doctors were still doubtful he'd survive—Brandon was holding Jaxon on his chest and talking to a social worker when a doctor entered the hospital room. "This is what a normal MRI looks like," the doctor said, holding up a film with an image of a brain. "And here's your son's." The second scan showed a yawning black space where the first scan had shown brain matter. The doctor then told us that Jaxon

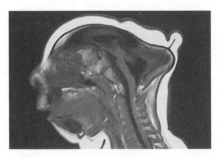

would probably never see, hear, walk, talk, or be able to tell us when he was hungry.

Just after delivering that devastating news, the doctor dropped a laptop and it slammed against a metal hospital tray. Jaxon instantly flinched at the sound. I lifted a brow, but the doctor didn't have a response. He simply turned and left the room. But the social worker smiled at me. "Well, obviously he can hear," she said. Brandon and I agreed.

We're so thankful that Jaxon can hear, because music stimulates all the senses, and that kind of stimulation will help our little boy grow and develop. I guess that means Brandon and I will just have to keep singing!

Look for the silver lining.

Norman Vincent Peale once said, "Watch your manner of speech if you wish to develop a peaceful state of mind. Start each day by affirming peaceful, contented and happy attitudes and your days will tend to be pleasant and successful." The apostle Paul puts it this way: "Fix your thoughts on what is true, and honorable, and right, and pure, and lovely, and admirable. Think about things that are excellent and worthy of praise" (Philippians 4:8). In other words: there is no cloud so dark it doesn't have a silver lining.

In Daytona Beach, Florida, right off the boardwalk, there's a restaurant called Ocean Deck. You're at home there whether you're dressed up or wearing a bathing suit and towel, and it's popular with the tourists. The atmosphere is fun and upbeat, with live entertainment every night of the week.

Brandon and I ate there a lot when we lived in the area. While we waited for our food, we'd look at all the out-of-state license plates tacked to the wall and read the sayings various people had painted above the booths. One saying has really stuck with us: "Pessimists complain about the winds, optimists expect them to change, and realists adjust their sails."

That's us. We are not Pollyannas, and we accept our son's condition. We are realists who choose to be optimistic.

We know that Jaxon will always be different from other children and that he may live a significantly shortened life. But we refuse to dwell on dark thoughts, and we actively look for the good things. He's alive! That's a miracle in itself. He can hear! That defied the brain scans and the doctors' predictions. He can see! We're not sure how well, but at the very least, he looks at us and smiles. He can coo and take steps and laugh! He has personality and a sense of humor. And he can love . . . oh, how he loves.

Brandon and I have learned that every day we have a choice: we can get out of bed with a positive outlook or a negative one. We can rejoice over our baby or fret over him. We can focus on the compassion and support we receive from the online community, or we can fixate on those who refuse to value Jaxon as the precious soul he is.

We have decided to be positive. We have decided to smile, to welcome questions, and to let the world share our joy in Jaxon's victories over his many challenges. We aren't seeking fame (though we do hope Jaxon's story spreads to everyone who needs an example of hope and courage). I don't care if people know my face or name, but I do care about giving a smile, a dose of encouragement, and most of all, hope.

So how do Brandon and I maintain a positive outlook in the midst of so many challenges? How can we keep hope alive when the world itself is roiling with turmoil?

We trust in God. And every day we spend some time focusing on Him through prayer and reading His Word. "Don't copy the behavior and customs of this world," the apostle Paul writes, "but let God transform you into a new person by changing the way you think. Then you will learn to know God's will for you, which is good and pleasing and perfect" (Romans 12:2). We aren't preachy when we post things online, and we don't condemn anyone who holds opposing positions, but we are guided by this principle: "If someone asks about your Christian hope, always be ready to explain it" (1 Peter 3:15).

In a nutshell, we are positive because our hope rests in Jesus Christ.

While we appreciate medical research and skilled doctors, our hope doesn't rest in medical professionals or the health care system. It doesn't lie in genetic research or in some nameless fate. Our hope rests in God, who has prepared a life for us beyond this one and who gives us strength and patience and courage every day to walk the path He laid out for us.

Keep on learning.

Looking back on Jaxon's first year, we never dreamed that we could learn so much in such a short time. When the doctors began to mention conditions and symptoms and situations we'd never heard of, Brandon and I started learning as much as we could. We believe that knowledge is power, and fortunately, knowledge is more accessible now than it has ever been.

When our journey with Jaxon began, we had never heard of Joubert syndrome or microhydranencephaly or GoFundMe. We knew nothing about caring for children with special needs, and we didn't have any firsthand knowledge of families who were raising children with physical challenges.

Although we've learned a lot in the past couple of years,

we're still learning. We're meeting more parents like us and more unique children like Jaxon. The knowledge we've gleaned, both from our own research and from talking with other parents, has helped us move from petrified and clueless to knowledgeable and experienced.

We hope that Jaxon will be able to help the medical community in some way. In an article on Discovery.com, Dr. Marc Patterson, a professor of neurology, pediatrics, and medical genetics at the Mayo Clinic, shared these words about Jaxon: "Children with these sorts of problems can help us rethink the role of the brain stem and the cortex in consciousness."[2]

Dr. Ganeshwaran H. Mochida, an assistant professor of pediatrics at Harvard Medical School and a staff physician at the Division of Genetics and Genomics at Boston Children's Hospital, says he is often amazed when he looks at a brain scan of children like Jaxon and then watches those kids outperform expectations. "Learning from each child is extremely important and hopefully as we understand more about the molecular and genetic basis of brain development and function, we will be able to also care better for these children and present accurate information to the families." He added, "Even in a young child, if a part of the brain is damaged, sometimes the other parts can take over better than in the case of older children or adults."[3]

The quality that allows the brain to adapt is called neuroplasticity, and it is a true gift. According to Dr. Norman Doidge, researchers in neurology have shown that "children are not always stuck with the mental abilities they are born with; that the damaged brain can often reorganize itself so that when one part fails, another can often substitute; that if brain cells die, they can at times be replaced; that many 'circuits' and even basic reflexes that we think are hardwired are not."

He continues,

In the course of my travels I met a scientist who enabled people who had been blind since birth to begin to see, another who enabled the deaf to hear; I spoke with people who had had strokes decades before and had been declared incurable, who were helped to recover with neuroplastic treatments; I met people whose learning disorders were cured and whose IQs were raised. . . .

The idea that the brain can change its own structure and function through thought and activity is, I believe, the most important alteration in our view of the brain since we first sketched out its basic anatomy and the workings of its basic component, the neuron.[4]

As Jaxon progresses, we believe the medical world will benefit from his diagnosis, from the study of his rare neurological condition, and from his story. Brandon and I are learning a lot—including how much medical experts don't know about the human brain. We would love to work with the top neurological teams in the country, if not the world, to further the study of congenital brain issues. We don't want Jaxon's story to end with Jaxon; we hope that he will leave behind a legacy of helping others. We believe that God has a purpose for his life—for who he is, for what he endures, and for the fight he keeps fighting every day.

Jaxon's life is already a miracle . . . so we won't be surprised if we see more miracles as he progresses.

But your life is a miracle too. The fact that you are a living, breathing soul with a body composed of millions of individual cells is nothing short of incredible. Take a moment today to think of the things you've accomplished in your life—not just the obvious things but also the seemingly ordinary ways your life has touched other people. I wouldn't be surprised if you astonish yourself.

With God, nothing is impossible. Miracles are all around us. "Now all glory to God, who is able, through his mighty power at work within us, to accomplish infinitely more than we might ask or think" (Ephesians 3:20).

As you go through your day today, look carefully at the people around you and the world around you. You just might spot a few other living miracles too.

LESSON 9

You're Not Alone

Brandon
Don't forget that others are walking the same path.

The world has seemingly shrunk since we had Jaxon. Since the creation of the Jaxon Strong Facebook page, we have heard from supporters all over the world. We send navy blue Jaxon Strong wristbands to those who support us in any way, and that group now includes people on all seven continents, including Antarctica. He has supporters in all fifty states, and he has received stuffed animals and little toys from dozens of countries, including Fiji, Ireland, Great Britain, Germany, France, Australia, New Zealand, Brazil, and Argentina.

When we see photos of people wearing Jaxon Strong wristbands, we are reminded that the world can be a warm place. We're excited and humbled that Jaxon's story has created a community that will also benefit other children and families.

Due to the generosity of one Jaxon Strong supporter, we were able to take Jaxon to Disney World when he was about a year old. When we stepped off the safari ride at the Animal Kingdom, we happened to meet another supporter who was getting off the ride at the same time. She recognized Jaxon, and we had a friendly reunion on the spot. We have been amazed by how Jaxon has the power to bring so many people together from different backgrounds and walks of life.

Jaxon's story has especially connected with expectant parents who learn that their unborn child has been diagnosed with a condition similar to Jaxon's. One of the reasons we have decided to share Jaxon's journey is to give those parents hope and to encourage them to fight for their little ones. In e-mails and messages from these parents, I am often asked, "What did the doctors tell you about . . . ?" and "When did you know . . . ?" and "How did you deal with . . . ?" I read every message we receive, whether it's from a parent, a member of the media, or a long-distance friend who simply wants to say hello.

Brittany and I have willingly accepted this responsibility because we believe that if we can bring attention to birth defects like Jaxon's and encourage research into their causes, then perhaps we can play a small role in helping doctors find a cure or a means of prevention.

As of this writing, no one has discovered a cause or a cure for microhydranencephaly. We have heard from several families whose unborn babies were diagnosed with similar conditions, and so far none of those babies have survived long after birth. As heartbreaking as that is, *all* of those parents have told us that they don't regret their decision to go ahead with their pregnancies. "Even though our child lived only a few hours," they say, "we would make the same decision again for the sake of knowing our baby in those precious moments."

Earlier we mentioned the conversation we had with our doctor about Jaxon's ultrasound results. We asked three questions: Would this pregnancy put Brittany in danger? Would Jaxon suffer pain in utero? Would Jaxon suffer after birth? The answer to each question was no.

But what if the answer had been yes? Would we still have continued the pregnancy?

Yes. We would have done all we could to save our son's life.

At the time we asked those questions, our emotions were raw and we were unaware of the facts we needed to make an informed decision. In that moment, the conversation between a doctor and parents is crucial, and we believe doctors should detail every option available rather than immediately suggest termination. If they thought Jaxon would suffer after birth, for instance, why not inform us about methods of pain relief? If Jaxon was being stressed in utero, why not present prenatal treatment options? And if Jaxon would have died shortly after birth . . . still, he would have *lived*.

A little girl who lives for only a few hours still has a precious story, and she leaves a permanent imprint on the hearts of those who loved her. A little boy who lives only a single day is no less human or wanted or loved than the child who grows up and lives to ninety-nine.

We believe there is an important divine purpose in the miracle of Jaxon's life. More than three hundred fifty thousand Facebook members have joined with us to support him and cheer him on through every smile, every challenge, and every accomplishment. He has been featured in magazines around the world, and in October 2015 he was the subject of a prime-time segment on *Nightline*. That's not bad for a little boy who barely tips the scale at thirteen pounds.

And it's not just Jaxon who has a unique calling. We believe there's a divine purpose in *every* life. Including yours. Including your children's.

It can be hard to remember that sometimes, and that's why there's so much power in community. No matter what you're going through, it helps to remember that other people are going through similar experiences.

Recently a friend of ours was attending a conference in Maryland. She flew into the airport and arranged to meet another woman she didn't know—they were going to share a ride to the retreat center. As they settled in for the hour-long drive, they learned that they had a lot in common. Both had adopted two children, a boy and a girl. Both had struggled with raising those children. "My son has a condition you might not have heard of," the other woman said. "It's called border—"

"Borderline personality disorder." Astounded, our friend finished the woman's phrase. "My son has it too."

Who would have guessed that these two women who had never met would have so much in common? For the rest of the drive, they talked about their struggles in understanding and guiding their sons. As they pulled into the retreat center, our friend looked at her new confidant and smiled. "This isn't something we discuss with many people," she confessed. "Mental disorders are so misunderstood."

The other woman nodded. "That's why we joined a support group. We discovered that there are lots of people walking the same path we're on."

No matter what you are dealing with, you're not alone. Search for support, and reach out to others who will understand your situation and your challenges. There is strength in community.

No one gets a vaccine against pain.
When you're walking the floor with your sick child in the middle of the night, it can feel as though you're alone in

the center of the universe and no one exists but you and the uncomfortable baby crying on your shoulder. Minutes stretch on, and an hour feels like a lifetime. Your nerves feel stretched to the breaking point, and even your skin hurts as you pat your child's back and whisper comforting words that bring no relief.

I've been there, and so has Brittany. We know that is a horrible place to be. You feel utterly helpless—and completely alone.

But you aren't. At that very moment, other parents are walking the floor, sitting by hospital bedsides, driving through the darkness, or searching for a runaway teen. Life brims with challenges of all kinds, and there is no vaccine against these painful experiences.

But the challenges, and even the suffering, are part of God's plan for us. "Dear friends," Peter writes, "don't be surprised at the fiery trials you are going through, as if something strange were happening to you. Instead, be very glad—for these trials make you partners with Christ in his suffering" (1 Peter 4:12-13).

When I became a father, the love I felt for the new little guy in my life was so powerful, so overwhelming, that for the first time I was able to grasp what God's love for His people must be like. As a kid, I'd heard that God loved the world so much that He sent His only Son to die for our sins. But how can a kid fully understand the breadth of that kind of love? How can a child understand the depth of Christ's suffering?

When Jaxon was born, I fell suddenly and instantly in love with my son . . . and I couldn't conceive of letting my son die for *anyone*. Clearly, God's love for humankind is infinitely deeper than my love for humankind. But oh, did I love Jaxon. And I hated to see him suffer.

With his curly blond hair and big eyes, Jaxon looks a lot like I did as a baby. He also has my strong will and stubbornness. When we try to get him to do something he doesn't want to do, he kicks his feet in protest. It's hard to get too upset about his little tantrums—partly because they're so doggone cute and partly because we're proud of him for demonstrating his determination and personality. So many people predicted that he would only sit in a corner and exist—that he wouldn't even possess consciousness. Others assume that because he lacks so much brain matter, he also lacks personhood and personality. But that's clearly not the case.

We know that many families have experienced situations worse than ours. They have children who can only respond to them minimally—or who can't respond at all—and our hearts go out to them. But that doesn't mean their children are any less worthy of care and love and dignity.

Some people ask us how we manage the nearly constant care Jaxon needs. We reply simply that he's our son, and we love him. But we're also grateful for the expression and emotion we can see in his eyes. Even though his speech is limited, he lets us know what he likes and doesn't like. I'm proud when I see that in some ways he is a "little me."

An original painting hangs in a hallway of our home, a gift from the artist. One of Jaxon's supporters saw a photo of me holding Jaxon against my chest—an image that was taken before we went to Boston, when Jaxon was in the "irritability phase." At that point, we could do nothing to soothe him. Brittany and I both walked the floor dozens of times during those months, and it was a challenging time. When that photo was taken, Jaxon and I were both exhausted.

After I posted that image on Facebook, one of Jaxon's supporters downloaded the image and reproduced it as a painting with the face of Jesus. The final portrait, which she sent us, is incredibly moving. In it you can see that Jesus is heartbroken over this little boy's pain, and it looks as though He would do anything to take that burden on Himself.

That's how I feel when Jaxon is sick. Any time we have to watch him get an IV inserted, have blood drawn, be put under anesthesia, or get an MRI—any time Jaxon has been frightened or upset—Brittany and I have watched with gritted teeth, fighting back tears. We'd do anything to be able to take away our son's pain and anxiety by bearing that burden for him. In times like those, being a parent is an exquisite torture.

Yet that is exactly what Jesus did for us. When He looks at us, He sees us struggling and reminds us that He loves us. That He has made a way for us. That He gave His life to bring us into fellowship with Him. And that He is guiding us through whatever trial we're enduring. He is with us when we're walking the floor or sitting by the hospital bed. He is with the father searching for the runaway teen. He is with the mother who weeps over a son whose problems spring from a disorder she can't understand or control.

We can rest in knowing that God is with us. We can close our eyes and rest in Him. Just as there's no greater joy for parents than to see their children happy and calm and content, there's no greater joy for Jesus than to see us abiding in Him.

In his letter to the Christians in Rome, the apostle Paul writes these words:

> Can anything ever separate us from Christ's love? Does it mean he no longer loves us if we have trouble or calamity, or are persecuted, or

hungry, or destitute, or in danger, or threatened with death? . . . No, despite all these things, overwhelming victory is ours through Christ, who loved us.

And I am convinced that nothing can ever separate us from God's love. Neither death nor life, neither angels nor demons, neither our fears for today nor our worries about tomorrow—not even the powers of hell can separate us from God's love. No power in the sky above or in the earth below—indeed, nothing in all creation will ever be able to separate us from the love of God that is revealed in Christ Jesus our Lord.

ROMANS 8:35-39

Before we had Jaxon, we never thought of death as imminent. Now we realize that no one has been promised tomorrow, so any day could be Jaxon's last. Or mine. Or Brittany's.

The psalmist writes, "Every day of my life was recorded in your book. Every moment was laid out before a single day had passed" (Psalm 139:16). God knows our birth date, of course, and He also knows our death date. He knows when He will call us home.

God never promised that this life will be easy or that

we'll get a free pass on suffering if we follow Him. But He did promise that whatever we face, we don't have to face it alone. He has given us people to walk beside us to share both the joys and the heartaches, and He has also given us His word that no matter how dark things get, nothing can ever separate us from His love.

Always Look Up

Brandon

Healing doesn't always come in the way we expect.

Brittany and I used to see God as the heavenly healer. Now we see him as the author of His perfect will.

After Brittany gave birth to Jaxon, we spent nearly a month in Orlando so we could be with our son as much as possible. The doctors' grim prognosis kept ringing in our ears, and it seemed clear that without some kind of healing, Jaxon wouldn't be able to live.

Those were rough, emotional weeks as we expected our baby to die at any moment. Except for the few times we went to the Ronald McDonald House to take a nap or a shower, we remained by Jaxon's side constantly in the NICU.

One day I slipped away to get cleaned up and sleep for a bit. I remember sitting in our room at the Ronald McDonald House, too drained to even cry. Alone in the quiet room, I stared at the wall and prayed aloud, "Heal him, God. Please give Jaxon what he needs to survive."

I went into the shower and leaned my hands against the wall, struggling to make sense of everything that had happened. The doctors had given us no hope; some had even suggested that he'd be better off if he passed away. Was that God's will?

I didn't know the answer, but I did know that for now, it was time to resume my vigil by Jaxon's bed. Days slipped by, and Jaxon didn't die. Although God might have done something to miraculously heal Jaxon's brain, He didn't. But that doesn't mean He didn't answer. I think He smiled when He heard that cry from my heart. Over time, the answer I've sensed in my heart is this: *It's okay, Son. Jaxon was meant to survive and reveal My glory.*

This can be a hard truth to accept: that God is sovereign over His creation and nothing happens that He doesn't allow. All things—good and bad—are under His control. The power of evil is not greater than God, nor does He stand idly by while destructive forces wreak havoc on earth. He is always good, even when things happen that are outside our limited understanding of what *good* means.

I came to realize—slowly, because I was a little shell-shocked from the emotional pounding we endured after Jaxon's birth—that God made Jaxon just as he is for a reason. God knows what His reason is, and I don't have to know. It is enough for me to love Jaxon, enjoy him, treasure him, and protect him for as many days as God loans him to me.

Once Brittany and I took our baby home, we stopped asking God to heal Jaxon, and we started thanking God for making him just the way he is. Now we see Jaxon as perfect. We are so used to the extraordinary shape of his head that when we see "normal" babies, they look a little odd to us.

When Jesus saw a blind man sitting by the side of the road, His disciples asked who had sinned. Was it the blind man or his parents? In other words, whose fault was it that the man was blind?

People have asked similar questions about Jaxon: Whose fault was it that he was born with only 20 percent of a "normal" brain?

Jesus answered, "It was not because of his sins or his parents' sins. . . . This happened so the power of God could be seen in him" (John 9:3).

We have watched God's plans unfold in a way we never expected. Jaxon was born exactly the way God intended so that through him and his story, God could touch people's lives.

I found the peace I needed when I stopped looking at

my ideas of what healing looks like and instead learned to look up.

Maybe you have been praying for a long time about some area of your life where you feel like you need to be healed or delivered. That's a good thing to bring the desires of your heart before the Lord, but as you do, keep your eyes open to how God may be at work around you and inside you. It just may be that God will bring healing—but in a different way than you would have imagined.

◦◦◦

Brittany
God has a good plan.

The mother of a child with a brain injury once wrote, "We would have called our daughter's handicap the greatest tragedy of our lives if it were not for the fact that through it we came to know the Lord much better. Words cannot fully express our keen disappointment when our little girl failed to experience normal mental development. Yet . . . the Lord knows that heartaches, if properly accepted, will enrich our lives in a way that could not happen otherwise."[1]

My prayers used to be simple. I prayed for other people and thanked God for this and that, and that was pretty much the substance of my prayers. But since having Jaxon,

I see God's hand every day and in everything. I see Him in people walking down the street and in the childlike trust of my son. I see evidence of His work in our lives in phone calls from friends and in e-mail messages from strangers. I see how He has touched people all over the world through Jaxon's smile, and I'm awed by the way He is at work.

We have claimed this Scripture verse for Jaxon: "'For I know the plans I have for you,' says the LORD. 'They are plans for good and not for disaster, to give you a future and a hope'" (Jeremiah 29:11).

That's what we believe. God has good plans for our son—both on this earth and in heaven. And He has good plans for you, too.

∽⊗

Brandon
You are more than a body.
In the past, I didn't spend much time thinking about the significance of a person's soul. I knew humans have souls, and I knew they're important. But aren't they just . . . part of us?

Yes and no. God created us as two-part creatures: a physical body plus an intangible element known as the soul or spirit. The physical part of our bodies came from the earth—God created the first human body out of ordinary clay. But the eternal part of human beings came from the Spirit of God.

When we're living here on earth, it's easy to focus on our physical bodies, especially since they are prone to yammer at us, reminding us that they need to be fed, rested, clothed, comforted, and exercised. Because our souls are out of sight, they are often off our radar, and few of us take the time to feed and refresh them. Our souls are the parts of us that yearn to know God and aspire to make a difference in the world. They're fed by prayer and meditation, and they're refreshed by things like music and beauty and art.

Because the soul is spirit, we shouldn't be surprised that no scientist or doctor has yet been able to locate the place where the soul resides. Those who don't believe in God often don't believe in the soul, and many people refuse to believe in anything that can't be scientifically proven. For those who doubt that the soul exists, I offer the following story.

In *Time* magazine, Dr. Scott Haig tells the story of a patient named David. David had lung cancer that had spread throughout his body and invaded his brain. As Dr. Haig puts it, "David's head was literally stuffed with lung cancer." David tried to be strong and cheerful for the sake of his wife and three children, but as the days passed, he grew weaker and eventually fell into a coma.

David's doctors did a scan of his head and discovered

that "the cerebral machine that talked and wondered, winked and sang, the machine that remembered jokes and birthdays and where the big fish hid on hot days, was nearly gone, replaced by lumps of haphazardly growing gray stuff. Gone with that machine seemed David as well. No expression, no response to anything we did to him."

One Friday night, Dr. Haig noticed that his patient's breathing had shifted to the gulping, gasping breaths that immediately precede death. David's wife was present, and as a nurse, she knew what those breaths meant. He left the room, but the wife followed and asked where her husband was. Obviously his body was there, but his brain was no longer functioning. And what about his mind and his soul?

Dr. Haig had no clear answers.

The next morning he checked David's room and found it empty. The bed had been freshly made, the floors had been mopped, and the area was ready for another patient. As he turned to leave, a nurse stopped him and told him what had happened the night before.

"He woke up, you know, doctor—just after you left— and said goodbye to them all. Like I'm talkin' to you right here. Like a miracle. He talked to them and patted them and smiled for about five minutes. Then he went out again, and he passed in the hour."

The doctor later confirmed the nurse's story with David's widow. Indeed, David had come out of his coma to say farewell to his loved ones.

It wasn't David's brain that woke him up to say goodbye that Friday," Dr. Haig writes in his article. "His brain had already been destroyed. Tumor metastases don't simply occupy space and press on things, leaving a whole brain. The metastases actually replace tissue. Where that gray stuff grows, the brain is just not there.

What woke my patient that Friday was simply his mind, forcing its way through a broken brain, a father's final act to comfort his family. The mind is a uniquely personal domain of thought, dreams and countless other things, like the will, faith and hope. These fine things are as real as rocks and water but, like the mind, weightless and invisible, maybe even timeless. Material science shies from these things, calling them epiphenomena, programs running on a computer, tunes on a piano. This understanding can't be ignored; not too much seems to get done on earth without a physical brain. But I know this understanding is not complete, either.

I believe that what Dr. Haig calls "the mind" is actually the soul, the nonphysical part of a person's nature—an element that defines us more completely than our physical bodies. Our souls are eternal, and they have strength that has nothing to do with muscles or brain power.

In closing, Dr. Haig writes: "Many think the mind is only in [the brain]—existing somehow in the physical relationship of the brain's physical elements. . . . [But] I cannot ignore the internal evidence of my own mind. It would be hypocritical. And worse, it would be cowardly to ignore those occasional appearances of the spirits of others—of minds uncloaked, in naked virtue, like David's goodbye."[2]

Recently I read about another man—a forty-four-year-old husband and father who was otherwise healthy—who went to the doctor complaining of weakness in his leg. After a brain scan, doctors discovered that the patient had only a "thin sheet of actual brain tissue" because fluid took up most of the space in his skull.

"It is hard for me [to say] exactly the percentage of reduction of the brain, since we did not use software to measure its volume," said Lionel Feuillet, a neurologist at Mediterranean University in Marseille, France. "But visually, it is more than a 50 to 75 percent reduction."[3]

How is it that this man is able to function and live a

normal life? I believe his "tiny" brain has adapted to his situation. I also believe that his spirit has given him the courage and strength to live the life his Creator intended for him.

Brittany and I will never pressure Jaxon to perform unrealistic feats, though we will encourage him to do as much as he is capable of. We want him to be as happy as possible. And we promise that he'll be loved as much as a child can be loved.

Our son may have very little brain matter in his skull, but he has every bit as much soul and spirit as any other human being on this planet. Brittany and I have seen joy light up his eyes and love soften his face. His little body makes him uncomfortable sometimes, but as an innocent child who has never experienced hatred or jealousy or resentment or greed, his sweet soul shows us a lot about what God's love looks like. And he isn't just loved by us; he also is much loved by God.

◦◦◦

Brittany
The evidence of God is all around.
We'd heard in church that God's love is all around us, but it wasn't until Jaxon came along that we understood that truth on more than an intellectual level. Now we've

experienced firsthand the evidence of God's persistent presence.

These days, if I see someone do something nice for another person or if I spot a mother who has a child with special needs at the grocery store, I feel like I'm in the presence of angels on earth. When I see Jaxon do something he's never done before or hear him make a new sound, I feel like God has placed a gold medal around his neck. Every little achievement Jaxon manages to accomplish is a gift from the hand of God, an unexpected blessing.

If we hadn't decided to give Jaxon a chance at life, I would be living the life of my choosing, focusing on my own plans and pleasures. Brandon and I would be working during the week, hanging out with friends on Friday nights, and wondering how to fill the hours on Saturday afternoons.

These days I never have to search for things to do. And I love that.

I'm in this blessedly difficult place and season because God has had a plan for me since before I was born. I can look back over my life and see how He has guided my decisions—even when I couldn't see that at the time. If I hadn't obeyed the nudge from God to move to Florida in 2010, I wouldn't have met Brandon, I wouldn't be married, and we wouldn't have Jaxon. That step of obedience

was the first link in a chain that has brought me to an extraordinarily challenging yet joy-filled place.

Brandon and I often feel like we are climbing a mountain in our attempt to love and care for Jaxon, and the path we're on hasn't always been smooth. But as someone once reminded me, we can rejoice when we see bumps in the road, because on the road of life, it's the bumps that we climb on. They are what teach us and stretch us. They challenge and strengthen us. And someday, when we stand at the top of the mountain and look down on the path we've traveled, those bumps will be so far behind us that they will seem inconsequential.

So we'll keep climbing. Because God is always with us and always leading us. Especially over the bumps.

◦∞◦

Brandon
Life is precious.
When Brittany first told me she was pregnant, I knew our lives were about to change forever.

I had no idea how *much* they'd change.

We had no way of knowing we'd have a son who would turn out to be so unique . . . or who would, in only a few months, touch more lives than we'd ever dreamed of touching.

We had no way of knowing we would soon explore the heights and depths of anguish, fear, confidence, and joy.

We had no idea we stood on the brink of an adventure that would test us, mold us, teach us, and challenge us for years to come.

Before Jaxon entered our lives, Brittany and I lived the lives of relatively carefree twentysomethings who didn't think much about death. We assumed we'd live until age eighty or so, and then we'd grow old and get weaker until we died. But now we realize that nothing has been promised to us, so we can't take anything for granted.

Now Brittany and I approach every new day as if it's going to be Jaxon's last. Even if our "big event" is going on the swings at the park or sitting outside so Jax can stare at the sky for a few minutes, we try to arrange some kind of enriching experience for our son. We focus on how he's doing and rejoice in the way he has anchored our family. I've even tattooed my arm with an anchor in Jaxon's honor.

Brittany and I have thought about what life will be like if and when we lose him. Selfishly, we never want to lose him, but we are also realistic. We will miss him terribly, and we will grieve, but we will do our best to make his life count in the service of others. In an effort to help other families in our situation, we've decided to donate Jaxon's brain to neurological research. His memorial service will be a time of celebration to remember everything he did, the lives he touched, and the courage he displayed. He has already accomplished so much more than was expected of him.

You may wonder how we can talk so calmly about celebrating after our son's death. Honestly, we wouldn't be able to if we didn't believe that God takes babies to heaven when they die. When King David's son died after only a few days of life, David rose up from the place where he'd been praying, got dressed, and asked for food—the first he'd eaten in several days. When his advisers marveled that he was returning to life as usual after his son's death, David said, "I fasted and wept while the child was alive, for I said, 'Perhaps the LORD will be gracious to me and let the child live.' But why should I fast when he is dead? Can I bring him back again? I will go to him one day, but he cannot return to me" (2 Samuel 12:22-23).

Our merciful, just, and compassionate God welcomed David's son into heaven just as He will one day welcome Jaxon. Just as He will welcome all those who have trusted Him.

The psalmist writes, "Precious in the sight of the LORD is the death of His saints" (Psalm 116:15, NKJV). Why does God consider our deaths precious? Because *we* are precious to Him. Bible teacher Arthur Pink writes, "The Lord loves His people so intensely that the very hairs of their heads are numbered: the angels are sent forth to minister unto them; and because their persons are precious unto the Lord so also are their deaths."[4]

The saints—those who follow Christ as their Lord and Savior—are the ones Jesus saved when He endured horrible agony on the cross. Because of His suffering, we can be cleansed from everything we've done wrong. That means death is not the end but the beginning of being united with Christ.

God considers a Christian's death precious because He is compassionate. When we weep, the Spirit of God groans along with us. Our God, whose love knows no boundaries, is aware of the suffering of all those who are ill, including babies and geriatric patients and those with limited brain function. And just as death is often welcomed by those who have been suffering for a long time, God knows that death is a welcome release for us because we were made for a better world.

At the hour of death—whether ours or a loved one's— God stands with us to strengthen, comfort, and help us.

As the old proverb says, "Man's extremity is God's opportunity." When no one can ease the pain of losing a loved one, God is with us. "Don't be afraid, for I am with you. Don't be discouraged, for I am your God. I will strengthen you and help you. I will hold you up with my victorious right hand" (Isaiah 41:10).

The apostle Paul writes, "While we live in these earthly bodies, we groan and sigh, but it's not that we want to die and get rid of these bodies that clothe us. Rather, we want to put on our new bodies so that these dying bodies will be swallowed up by life. . . . Yes, we are fully confident, and we would rather be away from these earthly bodies, for then we will be at home with the Lord" (2 Corinthians 5:4, 8).

I don't know what the future holds for us, and I haven't spent a lot of time worrying about it. Brittany and I are content to take one day at a time. But I know there may come a day when Jaxon's little body develops a complication it can't overcome. Brittany and I will do all we can, and we'll take him to any doctor who might be able to help. But if, in the end, Jaxon's strength is finally gone, Brittany and I will stand beside him, each of us holding one of his little hands, and we will weep as we pray for our son.

Then God, who is rich in mercy, will send angel escorts into the room—heavenly beings who will ease Jaxon's pain and calm his ragged breaths. His big, blue eyes will close, and his lush lashes will settle onto his cheeks as the angels summon his soul to heaven. I'd like to think that Jaxon's spirit will rise and swirl around us, blanketing us in the love and affection he tried so hard to communicate, and then he'll gently glide into the arms of the loving God who created him.

Brittany and I will look at each other, and even through our tears, we will smile. Because the death of such a loved one is precious to God . . . and because we were blessed to know and love Jaxon.

Sometimes I close my eyes and imagine what my first day in heaven will be like. If I die at an advanced age, I may marvel at the renewed strength in my supernatural arms and legs, in the sharpness of my eyesight and the crispness of my hearing. I may breathe in the sweet scents of pure air and growing things, and then I'll turn to see my loved ones—Brittany, my parents, my grandparents and great-grandparents, and so many friends I've lost over the years. Their wonderstruck eyes will meet mine, and we will laugh as joy bubbles up and flows out of us.

Then I imagine hearing a voice: "Dad? Mom?"

Brittany and I will turn, and we will see a young man— blond, with curly hair and wide blue eyes above a sweet smile. He will be standing erect, firmly planted on straight legs, his body fully grown to the size of a mature adult.

His face will shine in the light of the glory of God, and his head will be perfectly formed.

Despite the changes in his appearance, we will immediately know who he is. "Jaxon!"

Brittany and I will throw our arms around him and cover his cheeks and forehead with kisses, just as we do now. And he will bear up under all the attention with his usual sweet demeanor before turning and gesturing to a light gleaming on the horizon of heaven.

"All praise be to God," he may softly say. And we will nod with tears in our eyes as our throats clog with emotion. All the praise and glory and honor belong to God, for He not only sustained Jaxon and gave him a purpose on earth, but in His perfect timing He made our son perfectly whole.

A few months ago Brittany, Jaxon, and I sat on the couch in our living room and listened to a church service from The Rock of Central Florida, pastored by Rev. Steven Parker. We had heard that the church was planning to take up a collection to help support our family, and Brittany and I leaned forward in anticipation when we heard the pastor speak our names:

The Buells are very strong believers; they believe in the Father, they believe in His hand. . . . They have faith, and I look at you today, Brandon and Brittany and Jaxon, as you're viewing this morning from wherever you are—

From this house, we look to you today and we declare blessing in your life. Jaxon, in your body we prophesy strength, declare healing in every way; may every doctor you ever see be amazed by what you are able to do. Break the mold; don't let anybody define for you, Jaxon, who or what you can be. But by the glory and the anointing and the grace of the Holy Ghost of God, today we prophesy over you: your days are long, your purpose will never be cut short, and everything you are set to do will be accomplished. None of the fruit that was born in you will return void, but it will all accomplish that for which it was sent to the glory of God. . . . Amen.

Jaxon's life is precious, and we may never know the full impact he will have. Everyone deserves a chance to live, and everyone has a purpose. Jaxon has already touched and inspired more lives than most of us will in our entire lifetimes. Because of him, Brittany and I are better, we are blessed, and we are grateful. We are, quite simply, proud to be the parents of Jaxon Emmett Buell.

You may think that your life is ordinary, that you don't have anything special to offer. But you are created in God's image, and He has good plans specifically for you. As you look around your world, how can you encourage or inspire those in your circle of influence? Every day, wherever you are, you have the opportunity to be a light and a blessing. As Paul wrote to Timothy, "Be an example to all believers in what you say, in the way you live, in your love, your faith, and your purity" (1 Timothy 4:12).

Life will no doubt throw you a curveball at some point, if it hasn't already. When that time comes, we hope you'll be able to find inspiration from Jaxon's life. Trust your gut. Embrace uncertainty. Live the life you've been given, not the one you imagined. Know when it's time to give and when it's time to receive. Celebrate the little things. Use your words carefully, recognizing the power they wield. Savor each day. Believe in miracles. Remember that you're not alone in this. And always look up. For that's where we find real strength.

Acknowledgments

We would like to thank:

Jesus Christ, our Lord and Savior
Our parents, family, and friends
Boston Children's Hospital
Winnie Palmer Hospital for Women and Babies
Arnold Palmer Hospital for Children
Ronald McDonald House Charities
Dr. Heather Olson
Dr. Carl Barr
Dr. Shaista Safder
Dr. Michael Baker
Damascus United Methodist Church
The Rock of Central Florida
The Potter's House (North Carolina)
Family Research Council
Garrett Bess

Akers Media Group

First Green Bank

Jacksonville Jaguars

Orlando Magic

Training for Warriors

Lauren Maxwell

Pete Mitchell

Vic Micolucci

Robert Nokley

John Wilmoth and Renee Harlan

The multiple foundations that Jaxon has benefited
from

The media outlets that have shared Jaxon's story

Jaxon Strong supporters worldwide

Everyone else who has helped Jaxon and our family
along this journey!

Notes

LESSON 2

1. "Facts about Anencephaly," Centers for Disease Control and Prevention, last modified November 9, 2015, http://www.cdc.gov/ncbddd/birthdefects/anencephaly.html.
2. Kathleen McGrory, "Long before Zika Scare, a Florida Family Learned to Live with Microcephaly," *Tampa Bay Times,* February 12, 2016, http://www.tampabay.com/news/health/long-before-zika-scare-a-family-learns-to-live-8212-and-love-8212-with/2265184.

LESSON 4

1. Robert J. Morgan, *Nelson's Complete Book of Stories, Illustrations, and Quotes* (Nashville: Thomas Nelson Publishers, 2000), 509–10.
2. "Dave's Legacy," The Wendy's Company, accessed April 5, 2016, https://www.wendys.com/en-us/about-wendys/daves-legacy.
3. Ibid.

LESSON 5

1. Paul Lee Tan, *Encyclopedia of 7700 Illustrations: Signs of the Times* (Garland, TX: Bible Communications, Inc., 1996), 1509.

LESSON 6

1. Claude Lanzmann, *Shoah: The Complete Text of the Acclaimed Holocaust Film* (Boston: Da Capo, 1995), 8–9.
2. Joni Eareckson Tada, *The Life and Death Dilemma: Families Facing Health Care Choices* (Grand Rapids, MI: Zondervan, 1992), 93.

3. Ibid.

4. Karl Barth, *Church Dogmatics*, vol. 3, part 4, *The Doctrine of Creation* (Edinburgh: Clark, 1961), 423–24.

5. John S. Feinberg and Paul D. Feinberg, *Ethics for a Brave New World*, second edition (Wheaton, IL: Crossway, 2010), 75–77.

6. Dudley Barker, *G. K. Chesterton: A Biography* (Lanham, MD: Stein & Day, 1973), 65.

LESSON 7

1. Robert G. Lee, quoted in Ray Ashurst, *No-Nonesense Life Skills* (Bloomington, IN: WestBow, 2016), 27.

2. Diane Langberg, "The Art of Bearing Burdens," *Reformation and Revival*, volume 13, bk. 2 (Carol Stream, IL: Reformation and Revival Ministries, 2004), 65.

LESSON 8

1. If you'd like more information on music therapy, visit http://www.musictherapy.org.

2. Sheila M. Eldred, "Baby with Partial Skull Reveals Brain's Flexibility," Discovery.com, October 15, 2015, http://news.discovery.com/human/health/baby-born-with-partial-skull-reveals-brains-flexibility-151014.htm.

3. Ibid.

4. Norman Doidge, *The Brain That Changes Itself* (New York: Penguin, 2007), xix–xx.

LESSON 10

1. Paul Lee Tan, *Encyclopedia of 7700 Illustrations: Signs of the Times* (Garland, TX: Bible Communications, Inc., 1996), 1509.

2. Scott Haig, "The Brain: The Power of Hope," *Time*, January 29, 2007, http://content.time.com/time/magazine/article/0,9171,1580392,00.html.

3. "Man with Tiny Brain Shocks Doctors," *New Scientist*, July 20, 2007. http://www.newscientist.com/article/dn12301-man-with-tiny-brain-shocks-doctors.

4. Arthur W. Pink, *Comfort for Christians* (Bellingham, WA: Logos Bible Software, 2007), 87.